CULTURES OF THE WORLD®

SLOVAKIA

Ted Gottfried

BENCHMARK BOOKS

PICTURE CREDITS

Cover: © Walter Schmitz/Bilderberg/Peter Arnold, Inc
AFP: 85 • alt.TYPE/REUTERS: 8, 13, 30, 31, 33, 34, 37, 51, 54, 55, 64, 65, 67, 72, 80, 81, 84, 86, 87, 112, 114, 118, 119, 120, 122 • ANA Press Agency: 10, 11, 15, 18, 32, 39, 40, 45, 48, 50, 57, 58, 59, 61, 62, 76, 98, 113, 121, 127 • Camera Press: 23, 90 • Corbis Inc.: 20, 22, 24, 25, 27, 29, 41, 77, 83, 105 • Focus Team Italy: 1, 5, 12, 46, 49, 70, 104, 108, 123, 126 • Getty Images: 116 • Bjorn Klingwall: 78, 88 • Lydia Leong: 3, 4 • Lonely Planet Images: 19, 56, 96, 102, 103, 110 • MC Picture Library: 130 • photolibrary.com: 131 • David Simson: 9, 16, 43, 68, 71, 73, 91, 92, 93, 94, 95, 109, 124 • Liba Taylor: 52, 75, 128 • Liba Taylor/Hutchison Library: 6, 69, 101, 129 • Travel Ink Ltd: 38

PRECEDING PAGE
Young Slovakian girls in traditional costumes in the Tatra Mountains region.

Marshall Cavendish Benchmark
99 White Plains Road
Tarrytown, NY 10591
Website: www.marshallcavendish.us

© Marshall Cavendish International (Asia) Private Limited 2005
® "Cultures of the World" is a registered trademark of Marshall Cavendish Corporation.

Series concept and design by Times Editions
An imprint of Marshall Cavendish International (Asia) Private Limited
A member of Times Publishing Limited

Library of Congress Cataloging-in-Publication Data
Gottfried, Ted.
   Slovakia / by Ted Gottfried.
      p. cm. — (Cultures of the world)
   Includes bibliographical references and index.
   ISBN 0-7614-1856-3
   1. Slovakia—Juvenile literature. I. Title. II. Series.
   DB2711.G68 2004
   943.73—dc22   2004022241

Printed in China

7 6 5 4 3 2 1

CONTENTS

One of the main entrances
to the Bratislava Castle.

A view of some buildings
in Slovakia's capital city
on a cold winter's day.

INTRODUCTION

SLOVAKIA IS IN MANY WAYS a country in a time warp. Located in the geographic center of Europe, it is an independent country, little more than 10 years old, steeped in the history of empire and the traditions of the past. Its economy struggles to catch up with the rest of the industrialized world, while some of its people cling to a pastoral way of life that many in the modern world yearn to reclaim.

A landlocked state surrounded by the nations that once occupied or annexed it, Slovakia is a country of castles and rugged mountains. The people are religious, conservative, and proud of their heritage. They tend toward traditional speech patterns, customs, and folkways. Their reserve toward visitors often conceals a uniquely Slovakian warmth and humor.

Inevitably, the Slovakian way of life is changing. The robust terrain that characterizes this country is dotted with factories and power plants. Tradition is giving way to progress. Nevertheless, few places in Europe still offer so accurate a glimpse of past glories as Slovakia does.

GEOGRAPHY

MUCH OF SLOVAKIA RISES under pewter skies from two parallel branches of the western end of the fierce Carpathian Mountains. These are the High Tatras, or Vysoke Tatry, in the north, and the Low Tatras, or Nizke Tatry, in central and eastern Slovakia. It is a densely forested land, a harsh environment of primitive beauty.

LOCATION

Wedged into Eastern Europe and untouched by ocean or sea, Slovakia occupies a total area of 18,927 square miles (49,035 square km). Almost 80 percent of the country is close to 2,500 feet (750 m) above sea level. It has a 420-mile (677-km) border with Hungary to the south, and a 270-mile (441-km) border with Poland to the north, as well as a north-western boundary of 134 miles (215 km) with the Czech Republic, an eastern boundary of 60 miles (97 km) with Ukraine, and a western boundary measuring only 57 miles (91 km) with Austria. Slovakia's total land boundaries are 941 miles (1,515 km).

The High Tatras of northern Slovakia extend into Poland and reach heights of 7,917 feet (2,413 m). The highest peak, at 8,711 feet (2,655 m), is Gerlachovsky Stit. The Low Tatras of central Slovakia rise to about 6,562 feet (2,000 m). The mountain crags melt into hills and lowlands in the southern part of Slovakia, and dense forests give way to fertile farmlands. Here the mighty Danube River (Dunaj to Slovaks) flows past the capital city of Bratislava and runs along the border with Hungary.

At the base of the High Tatras, the Vah River—at 270 miles (433 km) Slovakia's longest waterway—joins the Danube to help define an agricultural area. Another such series of farmlands extends east into Ukraine. These regions are in pastoral contrast to the rigorous beauty of the peaks that dominate Slovakia.

Opposite: **A cable car at the Lomnice peak in the High Tatras range of the Carpathian Mountains in Slovakia.**

A man pulls a sled loaded with wood collected from a forest near the village of Vyborna in northern Slovakia.

SEASONS AND CLIMATE

Generally speaking, the seasons of Slovakia are rigorous, and sometimes cruel. The winters are cold and bitter, with freezing temperatures. Rainfall can be heavy in summer, particularly in June and July. In the High Tatras, summer temperatures can verge on freezing.

The kindest weather is found in the lowlands in springtime. However, even there the balminess is offset by rainfall, which is good for crops but bad for tourism. Most spectacular are the autumn storms in the highlands, when thunder rebounds off the mountainsides and sudden lightning illuminates an otherworldly vista.

REGIONS AND CITIES

Slovakia is divided into eight regions. Each has the same name as the city that is its capital. The regions are Bratislava, Trnava, Nitra, Trencin, Zilina, Banska Bystrica, Presov, and Kosice.

BRATISLAVA   The city of Bratislava, capital of Slovakia, is in the southwestern area of the country on both banks of the Danube River. Only 34 miles (55 km) from Vienna, it is a jarring mixture of Baroque architecture, Communist high-rise apartment buildings, and sprawling outskirts of what seem never-to-be-finished construction projects. But appearances can be deceiving; the central city is actually both cheerful and culturally exciting, with excellent museums, art galleries, and music of every variety.

Once a first-century Celtic settlement, today Bratislava has a population of over 438,000. Recently, restoration of the past has been in progress that includes the re-cobbling of ancient streets and the refurbishing and repainting of historic buildings. The ultramodern New Bridge that spans the Danube River typifies a new spirit of development by the citizens of Bratislava.

The Primates' Palace in Bratislava.

KOSICE The administrative center of eastern Slovakia, Kosice (ko-SHEET-sah) is a hub of industry, science, commerce, and culture. The area encompasses 2,607 square miles (6,753 square km), and the city provides services to an estimated 766,000 people. The city itself has a population of over 250,000. It dates back to A.D. 1230, and its historic center is known as the Urban Heritage Area because of its reconstructed main street lined with the mansions and palaces of well-off merchants from a variety of eras. Saint Elizabeth's Cathedral is considered one of the most beautiful Gothic structures in the world. It is the city's oldest landmark, built between 1378 and 1508, and features an altar with three magnificent statues and 48 panel paintings.

Kosice's main street, Hlavna Ulica, is lined by historical buildings and split down its center by a drain running through the city.

BANSKA BYSTRICA In central Slovakia, the district of Banska Bystrica (BAHN-skah BIS-trit-sah) is notable for the number of protected natural sites it encompasses, including the Low Tatras National Park, which at 313 square miles (811 square km) is the largest such natural area in Slovakia.

Slovakia's most popular tourist destination, Banska Bystrica offers both winter and summer facilities. In the cold-weather months there are many ski resorts for both alpine and cross-country skiing, as well as bobsled trails and lakes and ponds for ice-skating and ice fishing. During summer there are resorts devoted to swimming and boating, as well as the area's famous thermal baths.

The cultural hub of central Slovakia, Banska Bystrica is also notable for its architecture, and its churches and municipal buildings are not to be missed.

The main square of the city of Banska Bystrica has a spacious pedestrian area surrounded by historical buildings. At the top of the city's clock tower is an observation deck from which the whole city can be seen.

NITRA The region of Nitra (NYI-tre) sits on a low plain, separated from Hungary to the south by the Danube River. In addition to the city of Nitra, it encompasses the river port of Komarno, a trading hub for all of Europe. The area covers 2,450 square miles (6,343 square km) and includes the two nature reserves of Zobor, both of which are famous for their plant and animal life.

The city of Nitra is one of the oldest settlements in Slovakia and had been both the bishopric of the Great Moravian Empire and the site of the first Christian church in the country. It offers a rich cultural life, and there are regular exhibitions and concerts by artists and musicians from all over Europe.

A lone cow grazes in the peaceful plains of Slovakia.

TRNAVA Sometimes called the Slovak Rome, Trnava (TER-ne-ve) in western Slovakia is perhaps the most intellectual of Slovakia's regions. A center for religious study in the 13th century, the city has had a university since the 17th century. The region is known for its mineral springs and medicinal baths. The well-known spa resort at Piestany is only 22 miles (35 km) from the city.

TRENCIN The district of Trencin (tren-CHEEN) in the valley of the Vah River is one of the more pastoral areas of Slovakia. With a climate more temperate than most of the country, its green, wooded trails are a favorite destination for hikers. Racehorses are bred in the district, and horseback riding is a favorite activity. The city, originally a Roman military colony, is guarded by a fortified castle dating back to the 11th century.

A herd of sheep passes by a cottage on a farm in the western Tatra Mountains, central Slovakia. Sheep farming is widespread in the region.

THE GOLD MEDAL TOWN

In 1986 the United Nations Educational, Scientific and Cultural Organization (UNESCO) awarded their Gold Medal for Monument Preservation to the town of Bardejov in the Presov region of northeastern Slovakia. The medal was given for outstanding efforts in preserving and maintaining artifacts of urban, architectural, artistic, historical and cultural significance. It recognized that not just the individual artifacts but the town as a whole constitutes a deliberately preserved monument to a creative and glorious past, a tribute to its traditions and physical beauty. This is an environment vanishing throughout most of Europe, but which Bardejov exemplifies.

Bardejov sits on the right bank of the Topla River, some 909 feet (277 m) above sea level. It has roughly 32,000 inhabitants, and is a center of local industry and sports as well as culture. It is a medieval site in every sense of the word, with fortified walls, restored iron gates, and guard towers attesting to its determination to hold off invaders.

The center of the city and one of its many attractions is Town Hall, which was built between A.D. 1505 and 1511. The structure combines elements of early Renaissance and late Gothic architecture. It is considered the first Renaissance edifice in Slovakia, and perhaps the first in Eastern Europe. With its high-stepped gables, pitched roof, staircase oriels, wall paintings, and coat of arms of the original building, it defines the town square as a giant step back into history.

Another reason that UNESCO honored Bardejov is because of the Church of Saint Egidius, which was built in the 13th century and rebuilt in the 14th century. Located inside are the shrine fashioned by the Bardejovian builder Mikulas, a new vaulting created by the royal builder Stefan of Kosice, and the extraordinary tower erected by Franklin Stemasech. It is considered to be one of the finest examples of late-Gothic architecture in Europe. The interior decoration includes 11 wing altars of the early Renaissance period.

The Humanist Gymnasium bears a plaque proclaiming *Erecto anno 1508* ("Built in 1508"). More grisly is the Lamp Column, a medieval pillar that once marked the spot where criminals were beheaded. These are only some of the many buildings and monuments maintained by the town of Bardejov in an ongoing preservation effort that succeeds in keeping the past alive.

ZILINA The region of Zilina (ZHIL-en-ah), located in the Low Tatra Mountains, has some of the world's most famous caves. It adjoins Poland to the north and the Czech Republic to the west and is made up of heavily forested valleys surrounded by mountains.

Not only spelunkers (cave explorers) but hunters and fishing enthusiasts are drawn to the region. The local dams—Oravska Priehrada and Liptovska Mara—have made the local rivers, the Vah and the Kysuca, ideal for water sports.

The city, the third largest in Slovakia, stands where the rivers meet, and its famous 16th-century Renaissance belfry, the Burian Tower, looms over them.

PRESOV The High Tatras are the site of both the district and city of Presov (PRESH-awf). Here, within view of both Poland and Ukraine, the snow-capped mountains offer breathtaking vistas of natural beauty. In the north of the area are two fortified castles from the Middle Ages: Saris and Kapusiansky. In the south, the elliptically shaped city of Presov is partially surrounded by fortifications and dozens of Renaissance-style homes. The town square with its Neptune Fountain is surrounded by classical statuary.

The village of Strba, established in 1928 at the foot of the High Tatras in the Presov region, has 4,000 residents.

The iconic New Bridge, with its UFO-like summit, is one of five bridges that carry traffic across the Danube in the capital city of Bratislava. The other four are the Old, Harbor, Lafranconi, and Kosicka bridges.

TRANSPORTATION

Slovakia's major cities are served by a variety of public transportation systems. Bratislava's buses, trams, and trolleybuses run frequently and connect the city with outlying towns. A national bus network serves most regions of the country with a regular schedule of transportation that is reliable and prices comparable to train fares. Bus travel is popular with Slovakians, as the buses are generally faster than the regional trains and run more frequently than the express train.

There are 2,278 miles (3,668 km) of Slovakian railroads. The Bratislava-to-Kosice route (stopping at Zilina, Trencin, and Poprad) is covered in five hours. All express trains between Budapest in Hungary and Prague in the Czech Republic stop at Bratislava. There are also four trains daily between Bratislava and Vienna, Austria, a trip of approximately one-and-a-quarter hours. Much of Slovakia's in-country shipping is done by rail as well as by truck. The railroad system in Slovakia is complicated by the use of rail in different gauges. The majority of the track (2,188.47 miles, or 3,522 km) is standard gauge, but there are also 65.87 miles (106 km) of broad-gauge line and 31.69 miles (51 km) of narrow track.

The road network of Slovakia extends over 26,527 miles (42,717 km), providing access to all but the most mountainous wilderness areas of Slovakia. Most of the roads are paved, including 178 miles (288 km) of expressways. Snow removal is a high priority, and every effort is made to keep roads clear in the most severe winter weather.

Slovakia has no access to the ocean, but there are active river ports at both Bratislava and Komarno. A thriving import-export trade is plied on the Danube and other rivers in Slovakia. Tourists may also enter or leave the country by hydrofoils, which regularly run between Bratislava, Vienna, and Budapest.

There are 37 airports in Slovakia, of which 20 have paved runways. Bratislava and Kosice are the major terminals offering international service. There are daily flights between the two cities. Flights from Bratislava regularly connect with all major European airports. Slovak Airlines is the Slovakian national carrier. Slovakia also has a heliport and 106.88 miles (172 km) of navigable waterways, all on the Danube River. In 2003 the country's merchant marine fleet consisted of eight foreign-owned ships, four bulk carriers, and four cargo ships.

HISTORY

THE HISTORY OF SLOVAKIA is like a terrible dream filled with warfare, hardship, and subjugation. To wake from such a nightmare is to embrace joy and liberation. For Slovakians, this awakening is nationhood.

Archaeological evidence indicates that in the centuries before 1000 B.C., various nomadic tribes of Slavic origin settled, moved on, and resettled areas of present-day Slovakia. In the fifth century B.C. the Illyrians and later the Celts established more permanent settlements. These groups were expelled by Germanic conquerors in 100 B.C. Attempts by the Roman Empire to dislodge the Germanic peoples were unsuccessful.

However, a mass infiltration by Slavs reached its peak in the fifth century A.D. By the sixth century, Slavs had overrun the area, and in 623 Slavic tribes united under the warrior Samo and established supremacy over the region.

Left: **A rock inscription dated 179 A.D. in Trencin, western Slovakia, declares a Roman victory over Germanic tribes.**

Opposite: **The Municipal Museum in Bratislava preserves the capital's history in its numerous exhibits, which include torture instruments used in medieval times.**

EMPIRE AND RELIGION

Territories of present-day Slovakia were annexed by the Great Moravian Empire in A.D. 833. The empire encompassed areas that are today central and western Slovakia, the Czech Republic, and parts of Hungary, Poland, and Germany. Lasting only a little more than 70 years, it nevertheless established civilization and religion in the area with lasting effects.

In 863 Cyril and Methodius Thessaloniki, Christian missionaries, implemented a successful program of Christianization that established the religious identity of the territory of Slovakia up to the present time. Determined that the Bible should be accessible to converts, Cyril Thessaloniki created the first Slavic alphabet and translated the Bible into the language of the people.

The Spissky Castle, near Spisske Podhradie in eastern Slovakia, dates back to 1209.

The Great Moravian Empire, however, became destabilized. There were murmurings of revolt and plots. Hostile Hungarian forces massed on the borders. The Moravian prince sat uneasily on his throne. Finally, in 907 the Great Moravian Empire fell apart, and in 1018 the Slovak region was absorbed into the Magyar (Hungarian) Empire, and existed as part of it for nearly 1,000 years.

GERMAN COLONIZATION

As part of the Hungarian Empire, the territory of present-day Slovakia enjoyed a certain amount of prosperity. A mining industry was established, and Slovak earth gave up profitable amounts of gold, silver, and copper. Trading relations were established with other countries, and exports of fur and amber resulted in a surplus that enriched the Slovak economy.

However, in 1237 savage Tatars invaded from the east, and the economy fell into a major depression. In an effort to drive out the Tatars and rebuild the economy, the rulers of Hungary recruited Saxon-German artisans to settle underpopulated areas of the Slovak region. It was the beginning of a German migration that eventually established them as the majority population in many mining towns.

In the 14th century Matus Cak, a charismatic warlord, led a rebellion against royal power. His forces controlled much of the country, establishing Trencin as a capital, until his death in 1321, when Hungary reestablished control. In 1514 Juraj Doza led an army of 50,000 peasants and led a second rebellion against Hungary, which was brutally put down. There followed a successful invasion of Hungary by Turkey. The former Hungarian capital was moved from Buda (Budapest) to Bratislava. In 1686 the Turks were driven out in a series of notoriously bloody battles.

Above: **A portrait of the Holy Roman Emperor Joseph II (1741–90). His reforms played a part in the development of the Czech-Slovak nation.**

Opposite: **Tomas Garrigue Masaryk (1850–1937) was a respected philosopher and statesman.**

MAGYARIZATION

The formation of the Austro-Hungarian monarchy under the House of Hapsburg in 1867 was both a blessing and a curse for Slovaks. Serfdom was abolished, and a school system for all Slovak children was established. However, much of the reform was undercut by a program of enforced Magyarization (Hungarianization) aimed at replacing Slovakian culture and language with Hungarian equivalents.

By 1907 Hungarian had become the only language permitted in Slovak schools. Protests by Slovak intellectuals at the systematic attempt to destroy their ethnic identity were squelched. As a result, a movement of both Slovaks and Czechs, who were also being subjected to Magyarization, formed to oppose Austro-Hungarian domination. This was the beginning of the push for an independent Czech-Slovak nation.

When World War I broke out in 1914, Slovak men were called up to serve in the Austro-Hungarian army. Many rebelled, and some joined with Czechs to form guerilla units whose activities tormented the Austro-Hungarian forces. Meanwhile, during the war there was a diplomatic campaign waged by Slovak and Czech nationalists to persuade the United States, Great Britain, and France to support the liberation of their lands from Austria-Hungary.

The result was that at the end of the war, Slovakia announced its independence from the empire and its incorporation into the independent nation of Czechoslovakia.

BETWEEN THE WARS

In October 1918, Tomas Garrigue Masaryk, a leading advocate of Czech independence, was elected president of the new Republic of Czechoslovakia. Present-day Slovakia was still mainly a region of small farms. Programs to establish an industrial base were initially successful, but in the 1920s mismanagement by Czech bureaucrats undermined them. A movement for a separate Slovak nation began to gain momentum.

The worldwide Great Depression of the 1930s hit Czechoslovakia very hard. The Slovak region suffered close to 50 percent unemployment. Opposition to the federal government in Prague was bitter and growing. The movement for the Slovaks to secede and go their own way was gaining popularity. Agitating for an independent Slovak nation, in the 1935 national Czechoslovakian election, Communist and right-wing groups received 60 percent of the Slovakian vote.

During this period, Czechoslovakia was plagued with problems. Among the area's large German population, groups of Nazi sympathizers were organizing. Speeches by German führer Adolf Hitler repeatedly laid claim to the Czechoslovakian area known as Sudetenland, located in Bohemia and part of Moravia. Once briefly part of Germany, Sudetenland had a large German population. The Germans of the Slovak region supported Hitler's right to annex Sudetenland.

WORLD WAR II

In 1938, over the protests of the Czechoslovakian government, Great Britain and France signed the Munich Agreement with Hitler, ceding Sudetenland to Germany. In March 1939, as German troops advanced from Sudetenland to invade the remainder of Bohemia and Moravia, and as Hungary, Germany's ally, occupied an area of the southern Slovak region, the Slovaks officially separated from Czechoslovakia and declared Slovakia an independent nation.

Hlinka's Slovak People's Party (HSLS) took control of the new nation, and the party's leader, Monsignor Josef Tiso, became, in effect, the dictator of Slovakia. Tiso and the HSLS had strong ties to the Nazis of Germany and immediately proved to be very much in sympathy with their policies. Strong censorship rules patterned after those of Nazi Germany were enforced. All political parties except the HSLS were banned. Political opponents were jailed and their families persecuted. A Jewish Code was implemented, and 73,500 Jews were rounded up and transported to Nazi concentration camps, where they were killed.

Resistance to Tiso and the Slovak Nazis built slowly within Slovakia. Finally, in 1944 the Slovak National Uprising (SNP) revealed the wide extent of opposition to the Tiso regime. The SNP was led by units of the former Slovak army and included many partisan groups that had been acting against the Nazis since the start of World War II. The SNP was so effective that Tiso was forced to call on German troops to deal with it, and even then it took two months to suppress the uprising.

Slovak refugees on their way home from Hungary in 1946.

THE SLOVAK HOLOCAUST

In March 1939, Monsignor Josef Tiso, the premier of Slovakia, was summoned to Berlin for a meeting with German führer Adolf Hitler. Tiso was told that Hungarian troops massed on the Slovakian border would invade unless the führer took over the protection of Slovakia. Tiso replied that he hoped the Slovaks would "prove themselves worthy of the führer's benevolence." Subsequently, the Treaty of Protection (Schutzvertrag), making Slovakia a satellite of Nazi Germany, was signed. Immediately, anti-Semitic restrictions were imposed on the Jewish population.

Not counting those living in Slovakian lands that had been annexed by Hungary, there were about 90,000 Jews (3 percent of the population) living in Slovakia in 1940. A two-pronged policy to Aryanize Jewish property and to isolate Jews from the general population was instituted. The policy was dictated by the German Nazis and carried out by Tiso and the Slovak People's Party, familiarly known as Hlinka.

Within one year, 10,025 Jewish businesses were liquidated and 2,223 transferred to Aryan ownership. Three large labor camps—Sered, Vyhne, and Novaky—were built, and able-bodied Jews were herded into them. In the autumn of 1941, a special order was enforced to clear Bratislava of Jews. They were sent to labor camps to join other Jews.

In February 1942, the Slovak government asked the German Reich for assistance in removing all Jews from Slovakia. The Germans complied, and charged the Slovaks 500 reichsmarks for each Jew deported. At first, only males who were able to work were expelled, but when the Slovaks protested that families should not be broken up, the Germans agreed to include women and children in the mass deportation. They had to reassure the Slovaks that the Jews would never return and that no claims would be raised against stolen Jewish property. Between March 26 and October 20 in 1942, 60,000 Jews were sent to the Auschwitz concentration camp in the Lublin area of Poland to be put to death.

Monsignor Giuseppe Burzio, a Slovakian Catholic, protested to the government. He wrote to the Vatican in Rome, calling the premier, Tiso, demented. The Vatican sent a message that the death trains must stop. Pope Pius XII personally intervened. Finally, the deportations were temporarily halted. However, in 1944, 5,000 Jews involved in the Slovak National Uprising were taken prisoner. Slovakia was now occupied by German troops, and 13,500 more Jews were deported to the death camps.

The Red Army liberated Slovakia in April 1945. Tiso was tried for treason, convicted, and executed. He had shared responsibility for the killing of 75,000 Slovakian Jews—83 percent of the Jewish population in the Slovak region.

PRAGUE SPRING

At the close of World War II, in pursuit of the retreating German Nazi army, Soviet troops overran Czech and Slovak lands. Czechoslovakia was reestablished as a nation after the war, and Slovakia was once again included in it. Communists backed by the Soviet Union took over the Czechoslovakian government in February 1948. The country's administration was once again centralized in Prague, to the detriment of Slovakia.

Many Slovak nationalists and others opposed Communist rule. They were dealt with harshly. Disappearances, torture, forced labor, and executions were common over the next two decades. In 1968 Slovak Communist Alexander Dubcek became party leader. The Soviet secret

Demonstrators outside the United Nations headquarters in New York demand "Freedom for Slovakia" in 1960.

police (KGB) reported to Moscow that Dubcek had counterrevolutionary tendencies and would pursue policies unacceptable to the Soviet Union.

Dubcek introduced a policy that he called "socialism with a human face." It set out democratic reforms such as political opposition, freedom of the press, and freedom of speech. There were public protests about the methods of the Soviet police and the beatings and torture in the labor camps. Citizens demanded an end to Soviet domination of their country. A Czechoslovakian revolution was stirring.

The Soviet Union stopped it. On August 20, 1968, a massive airlift dropped several hundred thousand troops and tanks into Czechoslovakia. Soviet planes filled the skies over Prague. Dubcek gave in to the Soviet demands. Democratic reforms were scrapped. The major radio station in Prague was silenced. All non-Communist political parties were outlawed. Non-Communists and liberal Communists were excluded from the government. The media were put under Soviet control. Soviet troops were permanently stationed in Czechoslovakia.

THE VELVET REVOLUTION

Dubcek was removed from power and replaced by another Slovak, Gustav Husak. The reform movement was effectively dead, and there followed a stagnant period in which a dreary status quo defined Czechoslovakian politics. Nevertheless, Slovakian territory fared better economically than did the rest of the country, and the 1970s and 1980s brought to the region a high degree of prosperity, albeit under strict Communist control.

In March 1988, Soviet premier Mikhail Gorbachev discarded the Brezhnev Doctrine, a policy that allowed the Soviet Union to intervene in the affairs of other countries if they deviated from Communist principles. This was the policy the Soviets had used to justify their occupation of

Czechoslovakia. There were demonstrations in Czechoslovakia against Soviet troops even as they began to withdraw. This was the so-called Velvet Revolution, which led to a temporary non-Communist transitional government and eventually to Czechoslovakia's first free elections since 1948.

The question of an independent Slovakia still hung over the country. In 1992 negotiations over a new federal constitution for Czechoslovakia deadlocked. Meanwhile, an independent Slovakian parliament voted for independence and elected leftist Vladimir Meciar as prime minister. Finally, on January 1, 1993, the Czechoslovakian federation was dissolved and the indepen-dent Republic of Slovakia was established.

A SLOVAK NATION

Western Europe and the United States were quick to grant diplomatic recognition to independent Slovakia. However, the leftist policies of Meciar and his authoritarian style of government sent the Slovakian economy into a tailspin. In March 1994, a parliamentary vote of no confidence removed him from office. A coalition government was formed, but a majority partnership of right-wing and left-wing parties once again named Meciar as prime minister.

Alexander Dubcek (1921 –92) was elected speaker of the Federal Assembly in 1989 and 1990.

At this time, the parliament had authorized the sale of enterprises that had been state-owned during the Communist rule of Czechoslovakia. Meciar canceled such sales and halted all efforts to privatize Slovakia's industries. He imposed penalties and threatened the closure of all newspapers and television and radio stations that criticized the government. In effect, he returned Slovakia to an autocratic leadership that adopted the restrictions and policies of Communism. Slovakia was criticized by U.S. president Bill Clinton and cited as a violator of citizens' rights by many human-rights organizations.

The 1998 elections ousted Meciar as prime minister. He was replaced by Mikulas Dzurinda, leader of the rightist Slovak Democratic Coalition (SDK). Dzurinda was faced with problems of an unstable economy, high unemployment, and ethnic tensions involving the Hungarian and Roma (Gypsy) populations. In an attempt to return to power, Meciar decided to run for president in the 2004 election. Eleven candidates ran in the first

Vladimir Meciar speaks to the media in Bratislava during the presidential elections in 2004.

round, on April 3. Only two candidates could advance to the second round. The contenders were Vladimir Meciar and Ivan Gasparovic. Gasparovic, originally an ally of Meciar, was the former speaker of parliament and head of the non-parliamentary Movement for Democracy. The two men had a falling out when Meciar omitted Gasparovic from the 2002 list of candidates eligible for parliamentary elections. On April 17, 2004, Gasparovic was elected president by close to 60 percent of the vote. He was inaugurated on June 15, 2004. President Gasparovic and Prime Minister Dzurinda pledged to work closely.

In 2002 the prime minister had opened negotiations to join the European Union (EU), and on May 1, 2004, along with seven other former Soviet-bloc nations, Slovakia officially became a member. This new status led to hope for an economic recovery. Slovakia has recently attracted two automakers to the country—Peugeot Citroën and the Kia Motors unit of Hyundai. Manufacturing plants are expected to begin operations by 2006. The new nation is looking to the future with cautious optimism.

Ivan Gaspavoric greets the crowd at the presidential palace after being sworn in as president in 2004.

GOVERNMENT

STILL TO SOME EXTENT in transition, the Slovakian government is currently a parliamentary republic. The National Council (Narodna Rada), or parliament, consists of 150 members who are elected every four years by popular vote. A number of political parties participate, and they are represented in the National Council in proportion to the number of votes they receive. The minimum requirement to be seated is 5 percent of the popular vote. Formerly, the members of the National Council elected a Slovakian president to serve as head of the government for a five-year term. The candidate had to receive a minimum of a three-fifths majority to be elected. As a rule, no single party would have had a three-fifths majority in the National Council, so two, three, or more parties had to join forces to agree on a president. The constitution was amended in 2002 so that the president is now elected by direct vote of the people.

Left: **An election official in Kosice fixes the national flag on a chalkboard in a classroom used as a polling station in presidential elections in 1999.**

Opposite: **The presidential palace in Bratislava.**

FORMING A COALITION

A coalition is formed by the parties in the National Council to establish a parliamentary majority and to choose a leader. The coalition will legislate, and the leader of this coalition will usually be appointed prime minister by the president. The prime minister will then suggest members for a governing cabinet to be chosen by the president.

The cabinet runs the various departments of government. With the prime minister at its head, it is a hands-on body enforcing decisions on a day-to-day basis. Before the constitution was amended to allow for direct election of the president, the prime minister was the most powerful figure in government, and the president was a mere figurehead. Seven political parties won seats in the 2002 elections. None won a majority. A coalition was formed that included the Slovak Democratic and Christian Union, the Hungarian Coalition, the Christian Democratic Movement, and the Alliance of the New Citizen. The coalition outnumbered Meciar's Movement for a Democratic Slovakia and retained Rudolf Schuster as president and Mikulas Dzurinda as prime minister. In effect, a tenuous reform government had taken over until the next elections.

STABILITY

Flaws in the initial phase of the democratization of Slovakia resulted in a periodic paralysis in the ability to govern effectively. Single-issue political parties sometimes blocked legislation, and deal-making to form coalitions often resulted in corruption. Intolerance toward Slovakia's ethnic communities was reflected in measures that discriminated against them. Discrimination against the Roma (Gypsies) was particularly widespread and existed in housing and education. The privatization of state-owned industries was often scarred by ethnic preferences, nepotism, and under-the-table payoffs.

Recently, in a policy statement aimed at smoothing its acceptance into the European Union, Slovakia acknowledged past and present mistakes and outlined programs through which these mistakes are being corrected. The current government has begun a second term of leadership, an indication of its ability to provide effective leadership with the widespread support of the Slovakian people. After several years of self-assessment, consultation with international advisors, and implementation of reforms in the areas of minority integration, national security, and defense appropriations, Slovakia was invited to join the North Atlantic Trade Organization (NATO), a significant indication of the political stability of the country.

THE JUDICIAL SYSTEM

The breakup of Czechoslovakia left Slovakia with a Communist judicial system riddled with injustices and heavily weighted against the individual in favor of the state. Immediate reforms were adopted, based on the Austro-Hungarian codes of justice. However, this was put in place at the same time as the policies of privatization of state-owned industries and

Opposite: **Prime Minister Mikulas Dzurinda, standing in front of a large television screen, announces the result of the national referendum on EU accession in 2003.**

35

LAWMAKERS AND LAWBREAKERS

Organized crime is a serious problem in Slovakia. Established ties to international crime cartels exist around the country. There are also violent rivalries between Slovakian gangs and crime syndicates from outside the country. Despite reform efforts, there is still much collusion between members of the government and lawbreakers, usually white-collar criminals. Various types of crime and government corruption are interconnected. During the Communist era, Czechoslovakia was used for the transshipment of Southeast Asian heroin bound for Western Europe. There were plants in Slovakia that produced synthetic drugs for the markets of Central and Eastern Europe. With independence and the fall of Communism, the illicit drug organizations in Slovakia turned their attention to the opportunities opened up by the scramble to convert the country to capitalism. There were some government contacts already at hand, and more were developed to cash in on the privatization program.

The bidding procedure was circumvented, and whole industries were taken over by front men for organized crime. Protection rackets, sometimes posing as private-security firms or as unions, extorted protection money from businesses. Jozef Majsky, one of Slovakia's top industrialists, described how widespread this corruption really was: "Bribery is one of the working methods of this regime, from the top down to the working man."

While much is being done to stop this today, the Slovakian public still regards most police, judges, and politicians as being on the take. As for Mr. Majsky, he applauds the reform efforts and believes they will help in time, but he still maintains a private army of 470 armed guards as protection as he awaits trial for his alleged ties to organized crime. Even as corruption in government is being prosecuted, crime in Slovakia remains a growth industry. With drugs and protection rackets being targeted, Slovakian organized crime has turned to such profitable enterprises as money laundering and prostitution. A new government initiative known as the Schengen Action Plan is being implemented both to ferret out the gangs operating in Slovakia and to stop international crime at the border. Organized crime is a worldwide problem, and Slovakia is only one of many countries struggling to deal with it.

creation of a small business economy. The judicial system, including judges, prosecutors, and lesser functionaries, was inevitably involved in this, and politics, not justice, was often the deciding factor in the decision-making process. In October 2001, a code of ethics for judges was adopted. It laid down the basic principles of judicial integrity. However, recent polls show that the public still believes the judiciary is corrupt. There is still a great deal of concern as to the impartiality, political leanings, prejudices, and honesty of Slovakia's judges.

There are 55 district courts and eight regional courts in Slovakia. The regional courts function as courts of appeal and also hear certain cases of overriding national importance. There is a supreme court and a constitutional court as well. The supreme court is the highest judicial authority in the country. It only hears cases that have first been tried in a regional court. It can annul decisions or send cases back to regional courts for a rehearing.

The constitutional court is an authority independent of the judicial system. As its name implies, it is set up to ensure that judicial decisions are in compliance with the Slovakian constitution. Both civil and criminal cases can be heard in all of these courts.

Policemen stand in front of a McDonald's store in Bratislava to protect it from crowds demonstrating against Slovakian NATO membership in 2002.

ECONOMY

THE SLOVAKIAN ECONOMY is still coming to terms with the legacies of the past. The government and the nongovernmental power structure exhibit great determination to improve the economy, and the international community has generally been cooperative, but progress is slow. It is simpler to enact and implement new programs than to undo those already in place. It is easier to adapt to political independence than to reconstruct a financial system.

SERVICES

In 2000 industry accounted for 34.1 percent of Slovakia's gross domestic product (GDP), agriculture for 4.5 percent, and services for 61.4 percent. Slovakia has basically a service economy. The service industry includes

Left: **A souvenir seller in Bratislava displays hand-made necklaces and name bracelets for sale.**

Opposite: **Crowds patronize the cafés and shops on Saint Michael's Street in Slovakia's capital. Saint Michael's Tower in the background offers a view of the city from the top.**

legal services; architectural, engineering, and construction companies; accounting and advertising firms; telecommunications enterprises; social services such as health care and education; wholesaling, retailing, and franchising businesses; railway and trucking firms; utility companies; and, most importantly, travel and tourism services.

The national government is actively implementing the development of tourism. Federal agencies, working together with local governments, have promoted Slovakia as a tourist mecca for skiers, cyclists, hikers, wildlife enthusiasts, and snowboarders. They have promoted tours of national parks, castles, palaces, and age-old churches. The wineries, the caves of the eastern region, and the rich cultural life of Bratislava are

A Slovakian shopkeeper cleans her doorway at the start of the day.

stressed in government-sponsored television ads, on Internet sites, and through franchise arrangements with international travel bureaus. Visits to Slovakia's many spas are encouraged by the government. The result has been that this small, relatively undeveloped middle-European country attracts half a million visitors a year, thereby swelling its population by about 10 percent.

A commercial street in Banska Stiavnica, in the south-central part of the country. The town is the oldest center for gold and silver mining in Slovakia.

BANKING

The National Bank of Slovakia (NBS) was established when the Republic of Slovakia came into existence on January 1, 1993. The NBS head office is in Bratislava, with branch offices and special organizational units around the country. Its mission is to determine the monetary policy of Slovakia, issue banknotes and coins, and control and coordinate the circulation of money as well as the borrowing policy and payment system between banks. Rather than profit, the primary goal of the NBS is the maintenance of a stable banking system and the creation of stable prices in the republic.

The governing body of the NBS is the Bank Board. It establishes the monetary policy and determines how it is to be applied. However, neither it nor the NBS as a whole governs the practices of other banks directly, unless they violate Slovakia's Banking Act. The NBS may loan money to banks at low, predetermined rates, but it may not provide loans to any other part of the commercial sector nor to the federal or local government of Slovakia nor to the general public. In this sense it is the bank for banks and not for the people directly.

Other functions of the NBS include establishing the exchange rate of the Slovak crown, or *koruna* (KAH-roo-nuh), in foreign currencies and trading in gold and other foreign exchange assets. The NBS can also issue securities in foreign currencies for business people and travelers. One of its most important duties is the granting of licenses for new banks. These may be Slovakian banks or their branches headquartered in other countries. In overseeing such banks, the NBS has the power to withdraw such licenses from institutions that do not conduct business following the rules set by the republic's Banking Act.

FOREIGN TRADE

Under Prime Minister Dzurinda, the Slovakian government has implemented competitive incentive schemes that have attracted many new foreign investors. Foreign direct investment (FDI) in 2000 alone exceeded total investment in Slovakian industry over the previous 10 years. Germany is Slovakia's major trading partner, accounting for about 25 percent of Slovakia's exports and 25 percent of its imports. By November 2001, Russia had become Slovakia's third-largest trading partner. Russia satisfies Slovakia's need for oil, gas, and nuclear fuel supplies. Slovakia's oil refining, steelmaking, and chemical industries are kept busy processing raw materials from Russia.

Slovakia's export markets are primarily the countries of the Organization for Economic Cooperation and Development (OECD) and the European Union (EU). Nearly 50 percent of its trade is with EU members. Although only 2 percent of its trade is with the United States, Slovakia has received most-favored nation status from the United States, where many of Slovakia's products can now be sold duty-free.

A fuel truck drives past car factories Autonova and Lada in Slovakia.

MANUFACTURING

Throughout the 1990s, Slovakia struggled to stimulate a sluggish economy. Signs of significant improvement were noted in 2000. That year, GDP growth reached 2.2 percent, foreign investment totaled $1.5 billion, there was a strong increase in exports, Slovakia was admitted into the international OECD, and progress was made in the privatization of the banking sector.

In 2002 the GDP increased by about 4 percent and totaled over $67 billion. Total exports added up to $12.9 billion. The Slovakian economy is still beset by problems of inflation and unemployment, but the overall picture for the country looks brighter now than at any time since independence. Retooled Slovakian industries are turning out metal products, electrical and optical apparatus, machinery, transportation vehicles, chemicals, synthetic fibers, textiles, earthenware and ceramics, paper and printing, and food and beverages, for both the domestic and the foreign market.

AGRICULTURE

Although about 30 percent of the land in Slovakia is arable, agriculture accounts for only 4.5 percent of the nation's GDP. Only roughly 9 percent of the Slovakian labor force work on farms, which produce grains, potatoes, sugar beets, fruit, hops, and meat products from cattle, pigs, or poultry.

A major economic aim for the government is to increase the agricultural production of small farms rather than build up agribusinesses. The government views the regionally balanced development of agriculture as necessary to maintaining the rural population, which is basic to the cultural character of the country.

Farmers and ranchers produce enough staple food for Slovakia to be considered self-sufficient. However, the reduction of government subsidies for agriculture and the country's general economic decline in the past decade have combined to raise the price of food in Slovakia. Privatization of collective farms has dramatically increased the number of farmers, from 1,000 in 1991 to 19,720 in 1994. However, many of these farmers practice subsistance farming on small farms. Additionally, ownership of tractors in Slovakia lags behind the neighboring Czech Republic significantly— 23,479 versus 96,716 in 2003—so large-scale farming is limited and employment opportunities in agriculture have declined.

Federal government policy states that ownership of undeveloped land suitable for farming will be transferred to the local rural government. Parcels of such land will be offered to local people to live on and farm. State programs will contribute to the irrigation of such land as well as to the prevention of soil erosion and the financing of seed and machinery purchases. A program of rural tourism will be integrated with the farm program as part of maintaining the cultural integrity of Slovakia.

A farmer leads his cows and cart down a road in central Slovakia.

ENVIRONMENT

NO MATTER which party is in power, the one essential issue that takes precedence for the government is the maintenance and development of the Slovakian environment. It is an issue above politics. It is viewed as the cornerstone to a sound economy, a stable society, and a healthy citizenry. It is written in Slovakia's constitution that every citizen has the right to a satisfactory environment, a duty to protect and improve the environmental and cultural heritage, and the right to timely and complete information about the state of the environment. Funds allocated to the environment pay for social programs to improve health and living conditions, and for projects to safeguard mineral resources needed for economic development, maintain the purity of soil, air, and water, and protect the ecosystems that are part of the national heritage. Toward these ends a National Sustainable Development Strategy has been devised to which all political parties subscribe. The strategy has been formulated in accordance with international environmental law and the principles of the European Union.

Opposite: **Visitors enjoy the view of the lake in Strbske Pleso, a tourist town in the High Tatras.**

PROTECTED WILDLIFE

Approximately 40 percent of Slovakia is covered by woodlands, mostly beech and spruce trees and a rich variety of shrubs. To preserve this ideal habitat for wildlife, the Slovakian government enforces laws for the protection of animals and imposes strict restrictions on hunting. Slovakia has also fought off the effects of acid rain and the encroachment of deforestation. Forests abound with all sorts of birds: pheasants, ducks, partridges, storks, wild geese, grouse, and avian predators such as eagles and vultures. Wild animals such as bears, wolves, and lynx are protected from hunters. In the Tatra National Park, marmots, otters, and mink roam free in the woodlands. The chamois, a mountain antelope, is an endangered species protected by law inside and outside Slovakia's parks. Once almost extinct, its numbers are now increasing, and repeated sightings have been reported by hikers. Slovakians are justly proud that the chamois' environment is protected.

FORESTS

Approximately 5 million acres (2 million hectares) of Slovakia—40 percent of the nation's land area—consists of forestlands. State forests make up about 40 percent of the forestlands. Half of the remaining 60 percent is owned by cooperatives. Private owners, municipalities, and churches own the rest. According to an agriculture ministry study, half of the total forestlands, covering an area of 2,471,044 acres (1 million hectares), suffered damage from air pollution in 2001. That was more than double the number of trees affected by air pollution five years earlier.

Air pollution and acid rain have resulted in defoliation (the premature loss of leaves from trees) in 16 percent of Slovakia's forests. Defoliation is the first step in deforestation (the dying out of trees in forests). A major cause of this pollution is industrial plants both inside Slovakia's borders and in neighboring countries.

When Communism collapsed in Czechoslovakia and the other countries of Eastern Europe, its shocking legacy was that large areas of forests were dying as a result of acid rain. In their hurry to build industrial societies that would equal those of the Western world, little

attention had been paid to problems of pollution. Prevention and safety measures lagged far behind production. In the 1990s, 14,000 Slovakian schoolchildren were recruited to survey the damage to the nation's forests. Their survey, as well as studies done by professional measuring stations, showed that forests were continuing to deteriorate because of pollution during the post-Communist years.

Even with Communism gone, the major concern of both the government and the people was the economy. With privatization, the profit motive and the need to create jobs fueled the push for increased production. As production increased at oil refineries, such as the industrial giant Slovnaft, and at rubber and glass factories, clouds of acid rain settled above the forests. Lacking pollution-reducing equipment, both government and private heating and power plants spread dangerous fumes over the woodlands. Efforts to shut down industrial plants continue to be hampered by economic considerations, particularly the ongoing high rate of unemployment.

Above: **The Mengusovska valley is a popular area for mountaineers.**

Opposite: **Visitors in the Tatra National Park survey a map of the area.**

49

A manmade walkway takes visitors through the Demanovska Ice Cave.

CAVES

A common heritage of Slovakia and Hungary is the Slovak and Aggtelek Karst, a plateau region of 800 caves and abysses that straddles the border between the two countries. Two-thirds of the plateau is in Slovakia. The Slovak caves are protected as nature monuments by the Act on Nature and Landscape Protection. Four of them—Domica, Gombasek, Jasov, and Ochtina Aragonite—have been selected as World Heritage sites by UNESCO.

The Domica Cave, close to the Hungarian border, is 3.15 miles (5.08 km) in length. It forms a single underground passage with the Baradla Cave in Hungary. An underground river, nicknamed the River Styx after the Greek legend, runs through the cave. Slender, quill-like rock formations up to 118 inches (3 m) long decorate the Gombasek Cave. Sometimes they cannot be seen because the cave is deliberately flooded as part of a project to direct the floodwaters of underground streams. Another part of the project is the creation of a barrier to separate the ice areas of the cave from warm air and water so that formation of the ice will be encouraged.

The Jasov Cave is a veritable art gallery of stalagmites and stalactites. Its series of chambers and galleries have been compared to cathedrals. Rocks have shaped themselves into pagodas, art deco turrets, and miniature castles. Small, cascading waterfalls polish natural stone sculptures to a high sheen.

Children play in a hot spring in winter in the village of Besenov in northern Slovakia.

FARMS

Pollution is also a major concern for Slovakian farmers. Much of it is due to past unsound management by large state-owned and cooperative industrial farms. Approximately 3.7 million acres (1.5 million hectares) of Slovakia's more than 6 million acres (2.5 million hectares) of agricultural soils are endangered by water erosion.

In addition, Slovak farmers faced one of the worst droughts to strike east-central Europe in 2003. The main area affected was in the southwest extending east through the southern lowlands along the border with

An elderly woman opens the door of a pig's sty in central Slovakia. Farm pigs in the country have since the late 1990s been affected by a contagious viral disease known as classical swine fever.

Hungary. This is the warmest part of the country, and the soil is rich. With relatively low precipitation levels, the vineyards and vegetable farms here were hit especially hard by the drought.

Between the mountainous north and the fertile south is the area known as potato country, where a variety of vegetable crops are grown. The area still suffers greatly from acid rain and other industrial pollution.

ECOLOGY TREATIES

Preservation of the environment is an ongoing battle in Slovakia. This was recognized by the National Council as early as 1994, when it passed the Nature and Landscape Protection Act. Since then the act has been enforced and strengthened in many areas. Slovakia's commitment to ecological maintenance and reform has been reflected in its ratification of international treaties to enforce cross-border protection of the planet's ecosystem.

Slovakia is a member of the European Ecological Network (EECONET), which monitors forestry practices, the agricultural use of land, water management, and the impact of tourism on local ecologies. Since 1994 it has been a member of the international Convention on Biological Diversity, as well as the UN-based Bonn Convention on the protection of migrating animals.

Slovakia also adheres to the Ramsar Convention protecting wetlands, the Convention on International Trade in Endangered Species of Wild Fauna and Flora (CITES), and the Berne Convention protecting Europe's wildlife habitats. Other environmental treaty agreements supported by Slovakia include the International Partnership for Sustainable Development in Mountain Regions, and agreements on air pollution, volatile organic compounds, and hazardous waste.

ENERGY

Meeting its energy needs has been a growing source of concern for Slovakia since it gained independence. It simply does not have the natural resources inside its borders to meet the energy needs of a developing industrial economy. The only domestic energy sources are low-grade brown coal and small amounts of gas and crude oil. These cannot meet the energy demand. Coal-burning plants also emit polluted fumes that impact negatively on the health of the people and on the ecology of surrounding areas.

Slovakia is dependent on imported energy that is provided by crude oil and gas pipelines. Seeking to develop alternative energy techno-

A public worker cleans the cemetery near an active nuclear power plant at Mochovce in Slovakia.

A Greenpeace activist fixes a banner at the German embassy in Bratislava in 1999 in protest against German corporate involvement in upgrading nuclear facilities near the Slovak village of Bohunice.

logies, seven nuclear reactors have been put into production. However, partly due to public reaction to the catastrophe at Russia's nearby Chernobyl nuclear plant, one facility has been shut down, and there are plans to close the others at a cost of $1.55 billion by the year 2030. This presents a grave problem, since 53.7 percent of Slovakia's electricity comes from nuclear generators, while only 30.3 percent comes from burning fossil fuel, and just 16 percent comes from hydropower (electricity generated by turbines that are driven by fast-flowing water).

To deal with this, a program has been started to develop electricity using wind power. Slovakia's first wind farm is working in Cerova in the western region, 50 miles (80 km) north of Bratislava. This provides enough electricity for Cerova and the surrounding area. Its downside is noise pollution from the wind generators, but steps are being taken to correct that. Similar projects exploiting wind power are in the works, and there is optimism that wind power, rather than nuclear energy, will supply much of Slovakia's energy needs in the future.

SLOVAKIANS

AS OF JULY 2003, the population of Slovakia was estimated at 5,430,033. The majority of the people (85.7 percent) are Slovak. The largest minority, 10.6 percent, are Hungarian.

Actual numbers of the Roma (Gypsy) population are difficult to pin down, because they are a transient group moving both within the country and across its borders. Differing estimates are that Roma make up from about 2 percent to roughly 6 to 7 percent of the people in Slovakia. The 2002 census recorded 90,000 Roma, but Slovakia's statistical office calculates the actual number as 360,000 to 380,000.

There are also small pockets—each making up 1 percent or less of the population—of Czech, Moravian, Silesian, Ruthenian, Ukrainian, German, and Polish people living in Slovakia.

Left: **Slovakians walking to church in the village of Helpa in central Slovakia.**

Opposite: **Young Slovakian women dressed in smart uniforms perform at a concert in Trencin, western Slovakia.**

FACTS AND FIGURES

In Slovakia, the highest 10 percent of the population earns 18.2 percent of the national income, while the lowest 10 percent earns only 5.1 percent. There are 3 million people in the labor force, but at 17.2 percent the unemployment rate is high. Services employ 45.6 percent of the nation's workers, while 29.3 percent work in industry, 8.9 percent in agriculture, 8 percent in construction, and 8.2 percent in transportation and communication.

More than 3 million Slovakians live in cities and towns, while about 2 million live in rural areas. The countryside consists mostly of farms, vineyards, and woodlands. There has been a steady decrease in the rural

Cutting firewood is an everyday activity for these Slovakians in the Tatras area.

population since 1985. The much smaller increase in urban dwellers does not make up for it.

A very slight increase in total population is predicted for the first 25 years of the 21st century. The estimated birthrate of the Slovakian population is 10.1 per 1,000 people, while the estimated death rate is 9.22 per 1,000. This slight increase in population may be offset by emigration.

Presently, Slovakia is a well-balanced country age-wise, with 70.5 percent of the population between 15 and 64 years old. While 17.8 percent is under the age of 14, 11.7 percent is over 65. The median age is 35 years. However, a steady decrease in the youngest population group is a source of growing concern.

Most Slovakians live in towns and cities, where the lifestyles are similar to those in urban areas in many parts of the Western world.

WOMEN

On average, the women of Slovakia are older than the men. Their average age is 36.7 years, compared with 33.3 years for men. Women also live longer, with an average life expectancy of 78.64 years, compared with a male average life expectancy of 70.44 years. Older women are unemployable, and since there are so many more of them than men, poverty in Slovakia has become a major issue for feminists.

Women make up 45.9 percent of the Slovakian labor force. The percentage of women with full secondary or university education is slightly higher than that of men, but women earn on average 25 percent less in each job category. Women are drawn to fields like education, catering, health care, social work, banking, and insurance, where they encounter a so-called glass ceiling that limits their ability to rise to the highest executive positions. Because of family and child-care duties, women are regarded as undependable and are the first to be fired when there are layoffs. The income gender gap increases between men and women as they grow older.

The government has moved to equalize the status of women with the status of men. Slovakia's labor code (2002) states that women have the right to equal treatment in matters of employment, such as salary, promotion, and training, and that work conditions and arrangements should reflect the family obligations of both women and men.

Parental leave has replaced maternal leave in the labor code, with benefits distributed accordingly. Now, every employee, woman or man, is entitled to 28 weeks leave when her or his baby is born. An employer must provide either a mother or a father with up to three years leave for child rearing. During the first 28 weeks, the employee, woman or man, must be paid 90 percent of her or his salary. After that, they are entitled to a flat-rate monthly allowance. There are extra benefits for single or divorced mothers. Slovakia has one of the most liberal parental-leave programs in Europe.

Nevertheless, there is some criticism. In 2001 the government adopted the concept of equal opportunities for men and women in keeping with the European Union's approach to gender equality. Women's groups protest that while it is a fine declaration, it is not being put into action. It would require the passage of the Equal Treatment Act, which the Slovakian parliament has discussed but not approved. The act, which covers broad areas such as race, religion, sexual preference, and women's issues, is opposed by the conservative Christian Democrats.

These two elderly women work as potato pickers on a farm in central Slovakia.

CHILDREN: A NATIONAL CONCERN

As in every nation, children represent the future of Slovakia. Growth, progress, and prosperity rest on their shoulders. The Slovakian government has recognized this with a series of legislative initiatives to develop protections for the rights of the child. Because children are a precious natural resource, those who do not have a satisfactory home environment are of particular concern.

There are between 5,000 and 6,000 *adopcia* (UH-dahp-tsee-uh), or orphans, in Slovakia. Their numbers are constantly changing. Both poverty and cultural traditions impact on these children. In large families

Young children in rural Slovakia look after their family cow on the road.

living below the poverty level, putting two out of 10 children up for adoption may seem harsh, but it also may be viewed by parents as the only way to give their children a chance for a better life. Sometimes Roma children are taken away, over the objections of their parents, by social workers who decide that they are not being provided for adequately. In such cases the parents, willing or not, lose all legal rights to their offspring.

The government's main concern is to act on behalf of the children's welfare. However, the government's actions often bring heartbreak to both parents and child. Therefore the government is constantly reappraising whether solutions that seem painful on the surface are for the best in the long run.

Slovakian orphanages for children up to age 3 are administered by the Ministry of Health. About 2,500 children ages 3 to 18 are housed in 56 orphanages run by the Ministry of Education and Science. Ten percent of these children are in the process of being adopted. The rest either have guardians who are not their parents or live in the orphanages and receive legal institutional care.

There are strict rules for those who want to adopt children. There is also a shortage of would-be adoptive parents for children over the age of 5 or 6. Until recently, non-Slovakian citizens were not allowed to adopt Slovakian children. However, on October 1, 2001, Slovakia became a party to the Hague Convention on International Adoptions, which allows adoption by citizens of countries that are members of the convention. The United States is in the process of joining the convention, and when that process is completed, U.S. citizens will be able to apply to Slovakia for permission to adopt Slovakian orphans.

Slovakian children benefit from a good public school system and universal health care. Eighty-nine percent of the children attend primary school, and 74 percent will enroll in college. The child mortality rate has dropped dramatically, from 40 percent in 1960 to 9 percent in 2002, due to improved water supplies, sanitation, and mandatory immunizations. Ninety-nine percent of Slovakian children receive vaccinations for tuberculosis and other childhood diseases.

Roma children are the exception to this health report card. Roma communities suffer from high levels of unemployment, poverty, poor sanitation and nutrition, and high levels of crime. Roma children are often segregated in poor-quality schools and suffer from discrimination, cultural stereotyping, and language barriers.

A Roma boy eats potato meal in front of his mud house in Svinia, a settlement 250 miles (400 km) east of Bratislava.

MINORITY REPORT

The European Union (EU) initially denied membership to Slovakia. Bigotry directed against ethnic minorities, specifically Hungarians and Roma, was cited.

Recently Pal Csaky, an ethnic Hungarian, was appointed Slovakian deputy prime minister for Human and Minority Rights, and relations between native Slovaks and ethnic Hungarians are improving. There are also programs aimed at bettering interactions with the Roma, but negative attitudes toward them are deep-seated and progress is difficult. "Romany (Gypsy) rights have become one of the most important issues in EU

A Roma woman carries wood from the nearby forest to keep her home warm in winter.

accession negotiations," observes Rals Dreyer, acting head of the EU mission in the neighboring Czech Republic.

It is believed that the Roma migrated from the Punjabi region of northwestern India to Central and Eastern Europe in the 14th century. Today, although their numbers are difficult to pin down, it is believed that there are more Roma in Slovakia in proportion to the general population than in any other country. Mostly they are concentrated in eastern Slovakia. Here, their traditions, culture, and way of life effectively isolate their communities from their neighbors.

This isolation is one of the causes of widespread prejudice against them. Anti-Roma assaults are common, and some Roma have been killed. The Roma live in constant fear of attacks by skinheads, and local police forces do little to protect them or to apprehend their attackers.

According to the Center for Reproductive Rights and the Center for Civil and Human Rights, during World War II the Slovakian government collaborated with the German Nazis to sterilize Roma. Most alarmingly, since the fall of Communism in 1989, there have been charges that 110 Roma women in eastern Slovakia have been sterilized by local doctors under orders from regional officials. The national government's Interior Ministry has sent a special team of investigators headed by women to investigate these charges.

The investigation is only one facet of the change in policy toward the Roma. Under the authoritarian coalition headed by Meciar, the government turned a blind eye to the persecution of Roma people. The solution to the so-called Gypsy problem, according to Jan Slota, head of the Slovak National Party, which was part of the government coalition, "is a small courtyard and a long whip." Answers to a poll regarding attitudes toward the Roma included: "Send them to the gas chambers,"

THE MILITARY

Slovakian opinion polls rate the armed forces as the most respected national institution. Slovakia's governments, often shaky coalitions, may come and go, but the military is a stable establishment and commands the respect of the citizenry.

Slovakia's armed forces consist of the army (*right, soldiers practice raising the national flag before a ceremony to mark the country's entry to NATO in 2004*); air and defense forces; home guards (territorial defense forces); civil defense forces; and railway armed forces, subordinate to the Ministry of Transport, Posts and Telecommunications. Since Slovakia is a landlocked country, there is no navy.

The military manpower availability (males ages 15 to 49) in 2003 totaled 1,484,950. The country's Force 2010 Long-Term Defense Plan envisions a professional, combat-capable force of 19,300 by 2006. Defense spending was slated to increase to 2 percent of GDP by the end of 2003.

"Back to India!" and "Kill them!" Thousands of Roma have fled Slovakia to seek asylum in Britain.

There is a genuine effort by the present government, headed by Dzurinda, to improve conditions for the Roma. Housing programs to rescue them from ghettoes and crude dwellings are underway. There is a major effort to reduce the number of Roma afflicted with tuberculosis. There are retraining programs to deal with high Roma unemployment. Most importantly, there are preschool and early-childhood programs to help Roma children who may have grown up speaking their own language rather than Slovak.

LIFESTYLE

SLOVAKIA IS A LAND of contrasting and evolving lifestyles. The dramatic economic and political reforms that have swept the country since 1993, when independence was declared, have led to many social transformations. The gap between urban and rural life has widened. Family life has changed. Increased poverty has resulted in a higher incidence of addictive behavior. As Slovakia moved from Communism to capitalism, influences from the West impacted upon traditional culture in a variety of ways.

According to a 2004 Eurostat survey, Slovakians are among the most pessimistic and dissatisfied members of the European community. Of those interviewed, 46 percent are "not at all satisfied or not very satisfied" with their lives, and 53 percent stated that their situation has worsened during the past five years. Although the independence that followed the end of Communism led to gains in personal freedom, it also ushered in a decade of stress brought on by the necessity to adapt to new realities.

Left and opposite: **Slovakians in the cities have a variety of comfortable outdoor spaces to relax alone or with friends.**

Wide open spaces and natural colors characterize the Slovakian countryside, where the pace of life is slower than in the urban areas.

RURAL AND URBAN LIFESTYLES

Many Slovakian families have lived for generations in small rural villages located in the midst of agricultural areas. Essentially conservative and bound by cultural traditions, the people here have had difficulty coping with changes brought about by the transition to a free-market economy in an independent Slovakia.

The living standard of farmers and agricultural workers has decreased dramatically. When state farms and farm cooperatives were abolished after Communism, many families were plunged into debt. Poorly educated and unskilled except in farmwork, rural Slovakians have had a very difficult time making ends meet. The Banska Bystrica region in the south-central area of the country is covered with forests and agricultural lands. Unemployment in this large area hovers around 25 percent.

THE LURE OF THE CITY Because of the lack of opportunity, young people in the rural areas have left in search of work. Many have permanently relocated to larger towns, where there is some industry, or moved to the Czech Republic. This has left many parts of rural Slovakia with an aging, impoverished population. In areas where the Roma live, the poverty is even more acute.

In urban centers, however, where younger people predominate, there is greater optimism about the future. Although students are adjusting to the fact that it might be difficult to find a job after college, they are also eager to study and to travel abroad. For the most part, they view membership in the European Union as a first step to greater prosperity.

In contrast, Slovakia's cities are built up and have little nature. But they attract the younger generation, who seek the many opportunities for employment and excitement that the high level of urban activity provides.

A COSMOPOLITAN GENERATION In Bratislava, where the population is growing daily, the city is packed with members of Slovakia's newly Westernized generation. A great deal of private investment has gone into renovating the capital city to attract tourism. Bratislava is booming, with new restaurants, a thriving café and bar scene, and an energetic cultural life. Kosice, the second largest city, also has a lively cosmopolitan atmosphere and a newly rejuvenated town square. There is significant industry in the area, which attracts Slovakians looking for a good place to live and work.

Slovakians are gradually increasing their connections to the international community as the government funds improvements to the country's

Slovakian youth at a university campus in Bratislava grab bottles of vodka from a hostess for a mass toast that set a new Guinness world record in 2001.

communications systems, including additional phone lines, fiber-optic cable, and digital equipment. Slovakia has 38 television stations, 95 radio stations, and six Internet service providers. Over half the people have radios, slightly fewer own televisions, and about one-third of Slovakians possess telephones. Although most businesses utilize email, only 16 percent of Slovakians own computers, and Internet use is hindered by cost and limited access to computers and telephone lines.

SOCIAL CHANGES

A strong family structure has always been an

Slovakians on a trendy street in Kosice.

integral part of Slovakian life, both in the city and in the countryside. Every Friday night, the trains leaving Bratislava are crammed with university students returning home for the weekend to help their parents in the garden or with the housework. The rapid pace of change has also impacted on the age at which new families are begun.

In the late 1980s male and female Slovakians married at 21 years of age on the average. If a woman was unmarried by the time she was 24, people considered her to be a hopeless old maid. Today, Slovakian men marry, on average, at 28.2 years, and women at 25.2 years. Economic uncertainties have resulted in a generation that focuses on career development before raising a family. Despite the rise in the marriage age, 50 percent of all brides are pregnant at the time they wed. Intense pressure from families often prevents a couple who are expecting a baby from exploring any option other than marriage.

THE STATE OF MARRIAGE The number of unmarried couples living together, however, has also increased, as has the number of single women raising children alone. Life for single mothers in rural areas is much more difficult than in a large town or city, where difference is more easily tolerated. In small, conservative villages, single mothers are looked down upon as immoral.

The rate of failed marriages has risen dramatically, with 41 percent of unions now ending in divorce. This is due, in part, to a greater sense of personal freedom leading to a feeling that one need not remain in an unhappy marriage.

Women are rebelling against the cultural expectation that they will perform all of the household and child-rearing tasks in addition to holding down a job. Many are no longer interested in cooking elaborate meals everyday from scratch. They resent the fact that most men do not help with the domestic work, and they are critical of the amount of time husbands spend drinking with friends.

SOCIAL PROBLEMS

The stress that accompanies rapid change has also led to a tendency to pursue unhealthy ways to escape from the anxiety related to job loss, drab daily routines, or concerns about the future. Compulsive gambling and alcohol abuse are on the rise. Slovakians spend a great deal of their income (half of what they spend on food) on slot-machine gambling.

Alcoholism is a problem that is made worse by a historical tolerance for excessive drinking in Slovakia. Alcohol consumption is deeply embedded in many traditional festivals and celebrations. Although the legal drinking age is 18, bartenders ignore this requirement and routinely serve underage youths.

Alcoholism in Slovakia afflicts people from different areas, different age groups, and different walks of life. This problem weakens relationships because it often leads to domestic violence and marital discord.

THE FUTURE OF THE FAMILY

Despite the changes that have occurred as a result of economic instability and social transformation, the concept of the family unit endures as a highly valued way of life. Slovakians still deeply believe that home and children are the paths to fulfillment and greater happiness. This devotion is symbolized by the way modern Slovakians continue to cling to customs

A three-generation Slovakian family.

A WEDDING CUSTOM

At Slovakian weddings, the fun begins at the reception after the ceremony (*above, the wedding party leaves the church*). When the couple arrives at the banquet hall, the manager greets the newlyweds by smashing a plate on the floor. The groom and bride have to scoop up the mess with a broom and dustpan. If they miss any small pieces, these are carefully counted to predict the number of children the couple will have.

At the reception, there is a great deal of eating, drinking, and dancing. The other husbands link arms around the groom. He is required to toast each man and then finish the bottle himself. All the women dance with the groom and the men with the bride. When the groom is not looking, the male guests practice the custom of *unos nevesty* (OO-nahs NEH-veh-stee) by kidnapping the bride and taking her to a bar or café, where everyone drinks and dances. When the groom locates his bride, he must pay the bar bill before the two can finally leave on their honeymoon.

that have always played a role at wedding celebrations. Treasured family wedding rings are still passed down to new brides through the generations. Parents continue the custom of walking brides and grooms down the aisle. At many weddings, the bride wears a *kroj* (KRAH-yuh), a folk dress highly decorated with sequins that is said to protect the newlyweds from evil spirits. After the fall of Communism, Slovakians were free for the first time in many years to openly practice their Christian religion. For Catholics and Protestants alike, the church is an institution that emphasizes marriage, promotes the value of committed relationships, and encourages husbands and wives to become dedicated parents.

A wedding ceremony in a church in the Slovakian village of Zdiar in the High Tatras.

RELIGION

RELIGION IN SLOVAKIA is to some extent influenced by traditional ethnic conflicts, competing moral belief systems, and shifting political realities. Over 70 percent of Slovakians identify themselves as church members, and about 60 percent of those embrace the Roman Catholic faith.

About 84 percent of Slovakia's citizens say they believe in God. This is surprising in that after 40 years under Communist rule, Slovakians have been able to shuck off the antireligious teachings of the Soviet satellite government and find their way back to the ninth-century faith of Christian missionaries Cyril and Methodius Thessaloniki.

The anti-Catholicism of the Communist government began in 1948. Besides actively persecuting the Catholic Church and its clergy, the government revived the traditional antagonism between Czechs and Slovaks. Slovakia was a more rural, conservative, and religious region than the Czech areas of the country.

Following World War II, the Czechoslovakian Communist Party flourished in Prague. It followed that when the Communists came to power, government authority over Slovakia was transferred from Bratislava to Prague. In 1960 a new Communist constitution deprived Slovakia of its right to rule itself and placed Prague firmly in control of the region. Anti-Slovak prejudice and anti-Catholicism were merged in policies that were both ethnically and religiously biased.

COMMUNIST RULE

Under Communism, atheism was the only permissible moral doctrine for the Slovakian people. Catholicism, which had long been the major Slovakian religion, was now an enemy of the Communist state and the chief target of the Communist government. The aim was to wipe out the

Opposite: **An elaborate facade inside the Church of the Merciful Brethren in Bratislava. The church was built in the 17th century and was used by the Jesuits and the Carmelites before the Merciful Brethren, who provided for the physical and spiritual needs of the poor in the city.**

Catholic Church in Czechoslovakia. The result would be far more successful in the non-Slovak part of the country.

However, two generations of Slovak children would be indoctrinated with antireligious, anti-Catholic, anti-God beliefs. More than a decade after the collapse of Communism in Czechoslovakia, 10 percent of the population still defined themselves as nonbelievers.

On the night of April 13, 1950, with Action K, the Communist Party's designation for the program to dismantle the Catholic Church in Czechoslovakia, all 216 Catholic monasteries in the country were closed. Some 2,400 monks from 28 orders were imprisoned in concentration cloisters. The following autumn, 12,299 Roman Catholic nuns were rounded up

An old woman visits a grave marked with a crucifix near Spisske Tomasovce, a village in eastern Slovakia, during the Easter season.

and their 339 convents taken over for use either by the army or by government institutions.

"They broke in with guns during the night, woke us up roughly and herded us into buses," recalls 76-year-old Redemptionist monk Josef Dolezal, a theology student in 1950. He considers himself lucky because "[under Communism] many others were sentenced to life in show trials, or lost their health in the mines of Jachymov."

Action K included the seizing of Roman Catholic seminaries and other church property, the suppression of church publications, police disruption of church services, and the arrest of most Slovakian bishops, several of whom died in prison.

Catholic nuns attend a Mass in the Cathedral of Saint John the Baptist in Trnava in 2003.

THE CARDINAL'S CAUSE

Cardinal Jan Chryzostom Korec (*opposite*) of Slovakia is a hero with a cause. As the nation's foremost fighter against persecution during the years of Communist rule, Korec risked his life countless times. Yet he champions the memory of former Slovakian president and Nazi collaborator Tiso, and celebrated a memorial Mass for the 50th anniversary of his death by execution.

Born into a Slovakian worker's family in 1924, Korec joined the Jesuit order at the age of 15, just as World War II was breaking out. As a young man, he fought first against the Nazis, and then against the Communists. On August 21, 1951, as the Communist war against the Catholic Church was reaching its peak in Slovakia he was secretly ordained as the world's youngest bishop by special dispensation from Pope Pius XII.

The reason for this exceptional consecration was to ensure church leadership for Slovakia as other bishops were killed or jailed. In order to perform the ceremony, Bishop Pavol Hnilica faked illness to gain admittance to the hospital where Korec, who was genuinely ill, was being treated. Following the ceremony, Bishop Hnilica, a fellow Jesuit, barely managed to flee the country.

"The [Communist] regime launched a frontal assault," Cardinal Korec remembers. "It liquidated diocesan seminaries, publishing houses, associations, and schools, arresting bishops and harassing lay people. Those were humiliating, demeaning times."

Clergy had to minister to their congregations secretly. Bishop Korec's official job under Communist rule was as a manual laborer at a chemical factory in Bratislava. In 1959 he was arrested for performing Catholic rites and sentenced to 12 years in jail. He was released during the 1968 Prague Spring reform movement and permitted to travel to Rome to meet with Pope Paul VI. Returning to Slovakia, he worked as a hospital chaplain until 1973, when a newly installed Communist regime once again barred him from functioning as a priest.

Nevertheless, he continued to risk his life by ministering to Catholics secretly while working at his duties as an elevator repairman. His apartment in a Bratislava slum was bugged by the secret police, but it has been estimated that he nevertheless managed to minister to some 60,000 congregants over the next two decades. He also wrote over 60 *samizdat* (SUH-mee-zhduht), or illegal religious books, and ordained 120 priests. For years he functioned in defiance of the Communist regime.

In the early 1990s, when Communism collapsed, the Slovak Catholic Church recovered and Cardinal Korec was recognized as the natural leader of the recovery. His philosophy shaped the official position of the post-Communist church. "The liberty of the individual has been foolishly overemphasized," he says, "but freedom, however vulnerable and imperfect,

is a thousand times better than slavery. This has been our crucial experience since the fall of Communism."

Cardinal Korec is undoubtedly the most admired clergyman in Slovakia, but his popularity with some Slovakians has been tarnished by his championing of the cause of Tiso. A priest from the Nitra diocese, just as Tiso was himself, Cardinal Korec feels he has a responsibility to clear Tiso's name. He insists that Tiso, far from being a war criminal, was the victim of "impossible circumstances." He believes that Tiso could not have prevented the fate of the Jews or the anti-Nazi guerrilla fighters by refusing to cooperate with the Germans, but that doing so would only have made matters worse.

Cardinal Korec is not alone in this crusade. Many Slovakians feel that Tiso was executed unjustly and that his reputation should be restored. However, others, including many Catholics, think he got what was coming to him, and are dismayed that Slovak Catholicism's greatest hero should take up the cause of the man they believe to have been Slovakia's greatest villain.

Jewish leaders at the European Rabbis' Conference held in 2000 in Bratislava.

FAITH AND COMPROMISE

Roman Catholicism has become the foremost religion in Slovakia. It is not, however, the only religion. The second largest group is the atheists, who make up roughly 10 percent of the population. About 8 percent are Protestant.

The estimated Jewish population of Slovakia is based on a number of academic studies. Organizations of world Jewry may count only those who actively belong to Jewish organizations or practice the Jewish religion. Most of the Slovakian Jewish population was wiped out in the Holocaust, and those who escaped, returning to Slovakia after World War II, may be reluctant to be counted.

There are several small pockets of other religions practiced in Slovakia. These include the Church of Jesus Christ of Latter-day Saints (Mormons), the Brethren Church, Islam, Zen Buddhism, and the Bahrain faith. All denominations, large and small, are involved to some extent in the politics of the country. One reason for this is that Slovakia's ruling governments are formed by consensus and compromise. Religion inevitably enters into these compromises.

Another reason is that while 60.3 percent of the population define themselves as Catholic, this may not in many instances reflect support for church policy. Only about 20 percent of Slovakians are practicing Catholics. Nonpracticing Catholics hold attitudes that run contrary to church policy, such as favoring birth control and abortion rights.

Local representatives of different religions in Banska Bystrica stand around Pope John Paul II during his visit in 2003.

EDUCATIONAL CONTROVERSY

On September 12, 2003, Pope John Paul II proposed that when Slovakia became a member of the European Union, "they should bring to the construction of Europe's new identity (EU) the contribution of our rich Christian tradition."

The Slovakian parliament responded by asking that the new constitution then being drafted by the European Union include a reference to God as a source of the basic values and religious heritage of Europe. However, when the European Union did not comply, the Slovakian government voted not to pursue the issue any further. It also let stand the Slovakian constitution, which does not mention God but only refers to the spiritual heritage of Saints Cyril and Methodius.

The New Citizens' Alliance (ANO), formed by parties in parliament, sometimes forms coalitions with other parties where religious issues are concerned. They do not always win victories but do sometimes force compromises that broaden legislation to include other faiths.

Most recently, a majority of 95 members of parliament voted to sign a much-disputed treaty with the Vatican to make religious instruction mandatory in Slovakian elementary and secondary schools for students ages 6 to 18.

Pressure from a coalition in opposition forced the passage of a second treaty allowing 11 other churches—all Christian—to offer such classes. This was only a partial victory. Liberals, left-wing parties, and non-Christian denominations are still opposing what they consider now to be church schools co-financed by the state gaining control over curriculum not related to church doctrine. The issue is basically unresolved, and likely to be so for the foreseeable future.

Opposite: **Pope John Paul II, seated at the foot of a large crucifix, celebrates a Mass in Bratislava in honor of two Communist-era martyrs in 2002.**

Below: **Thousands of people attend an open-air Mass in the Slovak town of Roznava in 2003.**

LANGUAGE

SLOVAK IS THE OFFICIAL LANGUAGE of Slovakia. It is one of the West Slavic subdivisions of Slavic languages derived from the Indo-European language grouping. Other West Slavic languages include Czech, Polish, Upper Sorbian, and Lower Sorbian. Slovak is very closely related to Czech, and much of the two languages is mutually intelligible. Spoken by virtually all of Slovakia's 5.5 million people, Slovak is easily understood by other Slavs as well. It is also freely spoken by Slovak minorities living abroad, mostly in the Czech Republic, the nations of former Yugoslavia, the United States, Canada, and Australia.

Opposite: **A colorful array of magazines and comics at a Slovakian newsstand.**

THE SLOVAK ALPHABET

a	sounds like *u* in but	í	like *ee* in cheese	š	like *sh* in she
á	like *a* in father	j	like *y* in yes	t	like *t* in top
ä	like *e* in pet	k	like *k* in kernel	ť	approximately like *tyuh*
b	like *b* in boy	l	like *l* in last	u	like *u* in put
c	like *ts* in bits	ĺ	approximately like *lll* (a "long l")	ú	like *oo* in choose
č	like *ch* in child			v	like *v* in very; like *w* in wind if before a consonant or at the end of a word
ch	like *ch* in Loch Ness	ľ	approximately like *lyuh*		
d	like *d* in dog	m	like *m* in mat		
ď	like the *dy* sound in dew	n	like *n* in now		
dz	like *zz* in pizza	ň	like *gn* in lasagna	w	like Slovak *v*
dž	like *j* in jug	o	like *o* in odd	x	like *x* in fox
e	like *e* in set	ó	like *aw* in saw	y	like *i* in sit
é	like *ai* in pair	ô	like *wo* in wonder	ý	like *ee* in cheese
f	like *f* in fan	p	like *p* in pool	z	like *z* in zone
g	like *g* in go	q	like Slovak *kv*	ž	like *s* in pleasure
h	like *h* in hat	r	rolled as in Italian		
i	like *i* in sit	s	like *s* in save		

A VOICE FOR THE PEOPLE

Language was key to the independence movements of the peoples ruled by the Hungarian Empire, including the Slovaks, during the 19th century. The Magyars (ethnic Hungarians), although only about 4 percent of the total population of the Hungarian confederation, insisted on the Magyarization of the country as a whole. This meant that Magyar culture became the established culture. Magyar lords owned most of the estates, while non-Magyar populations were mostly relegated to serfdom. The Magyar language was the language of the land.

A banner speaks the message of a mass protest in Bratislava's main square for "an economically independent Slovakia."

The empire's other groups, including the Slovaks, rebelled against this and, as a matter of ethnic pride, stubbornly persisted in using their own languages. However, these languages were not, for the most part, organized systematically, nor were they arranged according to strict grammatical rules. These languages, both in their spoken and written forms, were subject to local interpretations. Intellectuals who also considered themselves ethnic patriots were frustrated and came to consider language as the most important part of establishing and preserving their culture.

The formulation of a Slovak language was to become the life's work of Ludovit Stur. Stur was born on October 28, 1815, in the Slovakian village of Zay-Uhrovec (now Uhrovec). He was the second child of Samuel and Anna Stur. Ludovit Stur was baptized in the Evangelical Lutheran Church and received his basic education from his schoolteacher father. This included a thorough grounding in Latin that was the basis for his career in linguistics.

In 1827 Stur was sent to Gyr in present-day Hungary, where he became interested in history and proficient in Hungarian, German, and Greek. He continued his language studies at the Evangelical Lutheran Lyceum in Bratislava and eventually joined the Czech-Slav Society, which by the early 1830s was concerning itself with both language and politics.

To support himself, Stur gave private lessons at the lyceum, which was connected with the Czech-Slav Society. He established important contacts with foreign and Czech scholars, and in 1834 was elected secretary of the society. By 1835 he had become coeditor of the society's magazine, *Plody* (*Fruits*), which published several of his poems. In 1836 Stur wrote a letter to the leading Czech historian, Frantisek Palacky, pointing out that the Czech language had evolved into an incomprehensible tongue for Slovaks—particularly Protestant Slovaks.

A BATTLEGROUND OF WORDS

Stur proposed the creation of a merged Czecho-Slovak language in which Czechs would use some Slovak words and Slovaks would adopt some Czech phrases. The Czechs absolutely rejected such a compromise. By now Stur had acquired a following among Slovaks. It was decided to shelve any idea of merging the Czech and Slovak languages and to create a new Slovak language instead. The West Slovak language, derived from the Indo-European language grouping, would be the basis of the movement.

The subkingdoms of the Hungarian Empire were in rebellion against the Magyarization of their various cultures. Respective national independence crusades were an integral part of the different language movements. The situation grew even more complicated when in 1848 the Hungarian revolution against Austrian rule, centered in Vienna, combined the struggle to free the peasants from serfdom with attempts to establish a variety of independence movements with nationalistic claims.

The Slovak nationalists were part of the anti-Austrian forces during the Hungarian revolution and were opposed to the Magyarization the Hungarians wished to establish once they were out from under the Austrian yoke. Stur and other Slovak patriots were carrying on a campaign to establish a strictly Slovak culture on the bedrock of a newly created Slovak language.

As pride in Slovak culture took hold, there arose opposition to merging it with any other culture, particularly Czech. In May 1848, a huge public meeting was held in Liptovsky Mikulas, where an ethnic Slovak program known as the Requirements of the Slovak Nation was proclaimed, and it was widely accepted by the Slovak people.

This manifesto was backed by force of Slovak arms against the Austrians, the Magyars, the Czechs, and others. While Stur and his

Opposite: **A postal sign in Bratislava.**

Below: **Posters printed in Slovak advertise theater productions.**

supporters were creating a purely Slovak language, which gained surprisingly wide acceptance among the Slovak people, a Slovak-run government was formed.

It did not last long. Politics prevailed. In 1849 the Russians became involved and helped the Austrians defeat the Magyar revolutionaries. In 1851 Austrian emperor Francis Joseph abolished constitutional rule in Slovakia and imposed himself as absolute ruler of Slovakia. The crusade for Slovak nationalism had been crushed but not eradicated. The Slovak language created by Stur and his followers prevailed.

Efforts to stamp out the new language scored temporary successes, but there was a lack of either will or coordination to halt publication of works

The panes of this kiosk in Bratislava showcase a spread of newspapers and magazines.

in Slovak written by Stur and others. There were efforts to stop the teaching of Slovak in schools, but since most Slovaks spoke and understood it, the language prevailed. Today, Slovak is the language standard used throughout Slovakia and among Slovaks elsewhere. It is an accepted fact that Stur's battle for a Slovak language has been won.

Stur paid a price for his victory. He was not permitted to publish a newspaper in the Slovak language. He lived in the suburb of Modra (near Bratislava) under close police supervision from 1851 until his death in January 1856. Many of his poems are still in print, and Slovakian schoolchildren memorize them. They celebrate Slovakian nationhood, and they do so in the Slovak language that Stur created.

Slovakians chat at a café.

Ruthenians celebrate a wedding at an outdoor museum in Svidnik in eastern Slovakia. The Ruthenians speak their own dialect.

DIALECTS

There are three major dialects in the Slovak language: central Slovak, western Slovak, and eastern Slovak. Central Slovak forms the basis of the standard language.

Groups separated by Slovakia's numerous mountain ranges have developed regionally distinctive slangs, word-shortenings, and pronunciations. For the most part, these dialects are mutually understood, much like those in the United States: New Englanders and Alabamans understand each other, as do New Yorkers and Kansans.

Some of the dialects fade into a border-region terminology common to neighboring nations. Thus, some Slovak frontier dialects merge with Czech, Ruthenian, or Polish dialects, affecting both vocabulary and pronunciation.

Written in the Roman (Latin) alphabet, Slovak employs several special accents that can change the pronunciation of a specific letter. A modified Roman system of spelling has been adopted. Like other Slavic languages, Slovak has a complicated grammar. For instance, nouns are feminine, masculine, or neuter, and a noun may have one of six declensions (endings) to express gender, number, person, and case, or combinations of these.

A system of defining old information versus new information is peculiar to arranging sequences and defining emphasis in the Slovak language. Phrases containing old information precede those with new information or those that are meant to have more emphasis. Slovak has six short vowel phonemes (groupings of closely related speech sounds), one of which is hardly ever used. There are also five long vowel sounds and four diphthongs, which are used to provide an alternate sound for a vowel. Consonants at the ends of words are often silent.

OTHER LANGUAGES

While Slovak is the native tongue of 85 percent of Slovakia's residents, there are a number of ethnic minorities living in the country who speak other languages, including Hungarian, Roma, Czech, Moravian, Silesian, Ruthenian, Ukrainian, German, and Polish.

Hungarians are the largest minority, concentrated largely in the southern part of the country and making up about 20 percent of the regional population. Almost 600,000 Slovakians speak Hungarian.

The large Roma (Gypsy) community lives mostly in the east and speaks five dialects of the Carpathian Romany and Vlax Romany languages.

Czechs, Germans, and Poles live throughout the country, while Ruthenians live primarily in the east and northeast.

ARTS

NATIONHOOD AND ETHNIC IDENTITY have been the key influences on the arts in Slovakia throughout its history, including its roles as part of the Austro-Hungarian Empire and subsequently of Czechoslovakia, its short existence as a Nazi satellite, its subjugation under Communist rule, and its present status as an independent state. Each of these periods left its mark on the various arts of Slovakia. Each has been incorporated into the strong ethnic identity of those arts.

LITERATURE

There can be no denying the strong influence of Austro-Hungarian sentimentality on Slovakian literature. The so-called Stur period of Slovak fiction and poetry that followed the death of Ludovit Stur borrowed noticeably from the romantic genre of Austro-Hungarian writers. At the same time, there was a marked folk flavor to Slovak works that glorified the culture of the Slovak people.

A subtle Slovak humor marked works such as the stylish *Marina*, by Andrej Sladkovic. Slovak comedies were distinguished from the light, frivolous Austro-Hungarian works by the point of view of a minor character commenting with sly cultural overtones on the plot from a dry, tongue-in-cheek, lower-class Slovak perspective.

Sometimes, however, ethnic pride went too far for the Austro-Hungarians. Janko Kral, whose epics and poems were the most outspoken examples of Slavic romanticism, and who narrowly escaped execution during the 1848 revolution, was a thorn in the side of the government until his death in 1876. Today, Kral is a major literary hero of Slovakia.

Poetry and drama were important factors in establishing Slovak culture under Austro-Hungarian rule. Dramatists like Jan Chalupka and Jan Palarik wrote popular comedies that tweaked the sensibilities of the ruling establishment and their views of class, culture, and ethnic superiority. At the turn of the 20th century, the poetry of Pavol O. Hviezdoslav introduced the literature and pride of the Slovak people to the outside world. His work continues to be widely translated today.

After World War II, Communist ideology was heavily imposed on Slovak literature. The most famous Slovak work of the period was *Kronika* (*Chronicle*) by Peter Jilemnicky. *Kronika* is a brilliant and massive work filled with anticapitalist themes and heroic workers. The lower-class Slovak as hero continued to be a favorite character after the fall of Communism. Today, ethnic pride is celebrated with books featuring folk wisdom and village heroes like those in the stories of Bozena Slanickova.

MUSIC

The earliest documented work of Slovak classical music is *Bratislava Missl*, a religious piece that dates from the 14th century, written by an unknown composer. Heavily influenced by German and Italian music, Kaspar Plotze and Jan Schimbraczky were important Slovak composers of the 17th century, and Juraj Josef Zlatni and Anton Zimmerman were prominent composers of the 18th century. Twentieth-century classical composers include Alexander Moyzes, and his student Dezider Kardos, who wrote *Hero's Ballad*. The most renowned modern classical Slovak composer is Ladislav Burlas.

Slovakia has a rich heritage of folk music that began hundreds of years ago, when singers of heroic tales traveled from village to village to

The National Theater in Bratislava.

entertain the people. These melodies were passed down through the centuries. German and Hungarian immigrants also contributed their music to this folk tradition.

In the 19th century, classical composers began using elements of folk music in their compositions. When modern musicologists began to collect examples of folk music, they discovered that a rural style was common in the north and west and included bandit and shepherd songs. In the agricultural plains and valleys, wedding and harvest songs proliferated among the inhabitants.

Traditional instruments that folk musicians performed on include the *fujara* (FOO-yuh-ruh), a 6-foot-long (1.8-m-long) flute; the *fanforka* (FUN-fahr-kuh), a reed instrument resembling the clarinet; and bagpipes, called *dudy* (DOO-dih) or *gajdy* (GUHY-dih).

PAINTING

Prior to Slovakia's independence, the three major influences on Slovak painting and sculpture were Hungarian, Bohemian, and Communist. Elements of all three are still visible in works produced by Slovakian artists today. However, as they are combined and modernized, a new, uniquely Slovakian vision is beginning to appear.

Dating back to the 12th century, the earliest Slovak paintings include frescoes by anonymous clerical artists in the churches of Dechtice and Bina. The Spis region offers religious works spanning three centuries and culminating in the 15th-century panels of Levoca's Church of Saint James and Kosice's Cathedral of Saint Elizabeth. The old wooden churches of

Painted flowers on a 16th-century house along the main square of Levoca in eastern Slovakia.

eastern Slovakia offer some of the best Gothic paintings and icons to be found in the former countries of the Austro-Hungarian Empire.

Among the first painters of the Slovak Baroque school to achieve recognition were Jakub Bogdan and Jan Kupecky. They were succeeded by Jan Kracker and Anton Maulpertsch, who produced what are considered to be the most decorative Baroque works in Slovakia. They may be viewed in the Jasov Chateau of Kosice and the chapel of Trenianske Bohuslavice.

The flourishing of Hungarian art in the 19th century encouraged the Slovak National Revival, which saw Slovak painters branching out from religious subjects. Among them were Dominik Skutecky, who took as his themes the day-to-day activities of peasants and workers in the Banska

Graffiti brightens up a fence in Levoca.

Bystrica area. The revival also featured the colorful landscapes of Ladislav Mednansky and the uniquely expressive portraits by Peter Bohun.

SCULPTURE

Opposite: **A monument sculpture in Banska Stiavnica.**

Below: **A wooden sculpture in a village in the eastern Tatras.**

Sculpture evolved along with painting from the 12th through the 19th centuries. The movable, painted wood figures of the craftsman Pavol of Levoca are superb early examples of Gothic sculpture. Master Stefan of Kosice produced some of the first works in stone. His landmark sculptures may be viewed at the Cathedral of Saint Elizabeth in Kosice.

The leading sculptor of the early 18th-century Baroque era was Georg Raphael Donner, an Austrian who worked in Bratislava. His statue of Saint Martin and the beggar is the showpiece of the Saint Martin Cathedral in Bratislava. Both sculpture and painting in Slovakia enjoyed a rebirth encouraged by the Bohemian art movement that sprang up following the birth of Czechoslovakia after World War I.

Portrayals of village life and pastoral landscapes typify the work of artists of the period, such as Martin Benka and Ludovit Fulla. When the Communists took over, they encouraged Slovakian art that celebrated workers and the collective manufacturing process in order to promote the progress of the state. Typical of the style is the Red Army Memorial by sculptor Julius Bartfay, just outside Bratislava.

The immediate direction following the fall of Communism was something of a reaction to the period before independence. Stano Filko, who had been banned by the Communists, became prominent with works created by the juxtaposition and highlighting of military weapons and war supplies. A more autobiographical technique by young artists such as Klara Bokayova and Martin Knut marks an increasingly popular modern trend in Slovakian art today.

FOLK ARTS AND CRAFTS

Folk arts and crafts developed throughout Slovak history. They flourish today chiefly in the northeastern areas of Spis, Bardejov, Svidnik, and Humenne. Tools, kitchen utensils, musical instruments, and furniture are still made by hand with intricate folk designs.

Traditional folk dress is designed with complicated pictorial or abstract embroidery in gay colors. Fabric weaving, glass painting, and wood carving are popular in rural areas. The folk tradition of painting houses with bright colors can be seen throughout Slovakia. Some of these structures are decorated with carved or molded plaster. These traditional arts and crafts are handed down from one generation to another and are preserved by the government through museum exhibitions.

CINEMA

Slovakian film only emerged after World War II. When the Czech and Slovak republics were united, films were made with combined crews and are referred to today as Czechoslovakian films. In the 1960s several new-wave directors made important films that included Jan Kadar and Elma Klos's 1963 *Smrt si rika Engelchen* (*Death Is Called Engelchen*). They also directed *Obchod na korze* (*The Shop on Main Street*), an Oscar-winning film that dealt with the effects of Nazism.

In 1976 Dusan Hanak directed the first Roma feature, which depicted a love relationship between a Roma woman and a *gadjo* (GUH-dyah), or non-Roma man. During the Communist period filmmakers suffered from restrictions on their freedom of expression. Although Slovakians continue to make films, filmmakers are now hampered by reductions in government subsidies. Juraj Jakubisko is considered to be the most important Slovakian filmmaker working today.

JURAJ JAKUBISKO

Often referred to as the Slovak Fellini, Jakubisko has been directing films since 1967. Jakubisko was born in Kojsov in 1938. He graduated from the department of photography at the School of Applied Arts in Bratislava. He studied at the Prague Film Academy (FAMU) and graduated in 1966, when the Czech new-wave movement was flourishing.

Oddly enough, Jakubisko was not interested in becoming a film director initially, but wanted to train to be a cameraman. Growing up, he had been inspired by the camera work in classic films such as Orson Welles's *Citizen Kane* and Sergei Eisenstein's *Battleship Potemkin*. Of the more modern directors, Antonioni was his major inspiration. However, his application to FAMU required that he submit documentary photos of the environment in which he was living. This was impossible because at the time he was fulfilling his military service at an airfield where strict state censorship was imposed, and he would have been arrested if he had been seen with a camera. So in order to get into the film school, he applied to become a director.

His early films, produced during his time at FAMU, received several awards. Soon after graduation at the age of 27, he made *Christ's Years*, his first feature film, which symbolized a goodbye to youth and its illusions. It was with his second feature, *The Deserter and the Nomads*, that he began his practice of using Slovak folklore, song, and dance to evoke fables of love and death on film. He drew upon his childhood memories of life in the remote village of Kojsov. As with several other films, Jakubisko did his own camera work on *The Deserter and the Nomads*. His next two features established his international reputation.

While being praised abroad, Jakubisko was prevented from working on original film projects for nearly 10 years by Slovakian politics. After the Velvet Revolution of 1968, Dubcek, who had tolerated artistic freedom, was removed from power and replaced by Husak, who banned Jakubisko's completed films and caused work to be stopped on *See You in Hell, Friends!* During this period Jakubisko was assigned to work on several harmless documentary projects. Eventually he was permitted to film again, but when he rewrote a script about a positive Socialist hero (*Build a House, Plant a Tree*) to present a more complex main character, his film was again banned in his own country.

By the end of the 1980s, Jakubisko worked in relative freedom and made a feature that dealt with the Communist takeover after World War II (*I'm Sitting on a Branch Enjoying Myself*). Regarded as the most popular Slovak director of all time, Jakubisko faced controversy when he moved his production company to Prague in the mid-1990s. His reputation was nonetheless ensured when he released his most ambitious film to date, *An Ambiguous Report About the End of the World*.

ARCHITECTURE

The castles of eastern Slovakia are some of the finest and most spectacular examples of fortress architecture in Central and Eastern Europe. Spissky Castle, dating back to 1209, is located near the town of Spisske Podhradie. With its jutting parapets and angled battlements set against a craggy mountain sky, it is one of the most photographed structures in Slovakia. Other castles of importance that have been restored include those at Zvolen and Bratislava. Slovakia's first Christian church was built in Nitra in 833. It no longer exists, but Nitra's Saint Emeram Cathedral contains a tiny 11th-century Romanesque chapel that includes remnants of the early cathedral's structure. The oldest religious building still standing (1002) is the Romanesque remains of a Benedictine monastery located in Diakovce.

In small villages that stretch from Svidnik to the Ukrainian border, where the remaining Slavic people who were originally from Ruthenia still live, there are wooden churches representative of folk architecture. Most of the churches are Greek or Russian Orthodox and were built during the 18th century. Constructed chiefly of spruce with onion-domed towers, they are located in serene country settings.

Metal nails were not used in the construction, because they symbolized Jesus Christ's crucifixion. The churches consist of three parts: the sanctuary, the altar, and the nave, which represent the Holy Trinity. In each church is an iconostasis, a wall decorated with icons separating the sanctuary and altar from the nave.

Seventeenth-century Slovak aristocrats and wealthy merchants built their homes in the Baroque style and were noted for elaborate stucco work. This style is represented by the University Church of Saint John the Baptist in Trnava (1637). Architectural influences from Budapest and Vienna contributed to several structures erected in the Art Nouveau style in the late 19th and early 20th centuries. An excellent example is the Church of Saint Elizabeth in Bratislava, designed by the Hungarian architect Edmund Lechner. During the Communist era, many monumental structures were built, including the New Bridge in Bratislava.

Above: **The town hall in Levoca was first built in the 15th century, with paintings decorating its walls.**

Opposite: **The House of the Good Shepherd, a museum of 18th- and 19th-century clocks, is a beautiful example of Rococo burgher architecture in Bratislava.**

LEISURE

SLOVAKIA'S MOUNTAINS, rivers, and lakes offer many opportunities for outdoor activities. Skiing, hiking, cycling, and water sports are very popular. Serious spelunkers explore the beautiful caves that enhance the countryside. In addition, the large number of mineral springs has led to the establishment of numerous spas and health resorts located near spa towns, which locals and tourists alike visit during their vacations. As in many other European countries, soccer and ice hockey are the most popular spectator sports.

SPELUNKING

A network of over 3,800 caves weaves through Slovakia. The best-known ones have been declared national monuments. Only 12 are currently open to members of the public, who delve into them to see their intriguing formations.

The Demanovska Ice Cave, in the Low Tatras, was first written about in 1719. It is 5,742 feet (1,750 m) long with ice filling in the bottom. The Harmanecka Cave, situated to the northwest of Banska Bystrica, is home to nine different species of bats. A walk through the cave takes the spelunker through several tiny passages less than 1 yard (1.1 m) wide that open dramatically into enormous, spacious halls. A trip through the cave takes about one-and-a-half hours. This cave has been familiar to locals since ancient times.

SKIING AND SNOWBOARDING

From December through April, fans of snow sports flock to the High and Low Tatras. Some ski areas provide artificial snow at other times of the year. One of the most visited ski centers is Jasna, the largest area devoted

Slovakian Tomas Bulik (in white) celebrates a goal in a match against the Russian team at the Ice Hockey World Championship held in 2004 in Helsinki, Finland.

to this sport in Eastern Europe. Located in the Low Tatras National Park, Jasna is situated on the slopes of the Chopok peak. Jasna has been the site of several World Cup ski races. The High Tatras have many ski resorts, as does the Vratna valley in the Mala Fatra Mountains. Snowboarding has increased in popularity at ski centers, as the resorts have been improving their terrain to accommodate this relatively new sport.

WATER SPORTS

White-water canoeing and kayaking are enjoyed by hardy Slovakians in the spring. It is then that the swift streams created by the melting snows of winter flow down the mountains. Rivers popular for these activities are the upper Vah and the Hron. Located in the Pieniny National Park, the Dunajec River that divides Slovakia and Poland is heavily used by members of both countries for rafting.

Slovakia has produced several World and Olympic champions in water-sport competitions. Swimmer Martina Morakova, born in the small town of Piestany on the banks of the Vah River, won a silver medal in the 200-m freestyle and a bronze in the 100-m butterfly at the 2000 World Championships. In the 2000 Olympics rowing and water sports, Pavel and Peter Hochschorner, two brothers, won the two-man canoe gold medal.

White-water rafting on the Dunajec River.

Lubos Pavlik of Slovakia pushes his bike out of a snow bank after colliding on the track during a race in the central Slovakian ski resort of Myto pod Dumbierom in 1999.

HIKING AND CYCLING

Slovakia is a prime area for hiking. There is a network of well-marked and connected trails. These extensive color-coded trails are maintained by the Slovak Hiking Club, an organization that provides very useful hiking maps. The practice of marking and keeping up the trails began near the town of Banska Stiavnica in 1874. Recommended trails are of varying lengths and for different degrees of skill. The best hikes are in the High Tatras, Mala Fatra of central Slovakia, the Slovak Paradise, and the Slovak Karst in eastern Slovakia. All offer spectacular views of breathtaking scenery.

Many Slovakians are avid cyclists. Mountain bikes are the equipment of choice for this sport, as most trails are very hilly. There is a well-known biking route that links Bratislava with Vienna, Austria.

SPAS

Hundreds of mineral springs dot the Slovakian landscape. Spas that promote health and encourage relaxation are located near these springs. The Roman legions of Emperor Marcus Aurelius, who ruled the Roman Empire from A.D. 161 to 180, bathed in the springs when they came through the area that is now Slovakia.

Thermal springs and mud baths are believed by some to cure and prevent illnesses and to prolong life. Near the springs are large deposits of healing mud and peat, which are applied to the body during spa visits. Many of the waters have been designated for healing specific ailments. Bardejovske Kupele, a spa in Bardejov in eastern Slovakia, is noted for curing stomach problems and respiratory diseases. The Piestany Spa in western Slovakia is visited by those seeking treatment for rheumatism and nervous disorders.

THE PIESTANY SPA

Located northeast of Bratislava, the Piestany Spa has a long history of treating rheumatic illnesses. Archaeologists date settlers in this area as far back as 80,000 years ago. Celtic, Germanic, and old Slavic civilizations made use of the curative waters. Many prominent medical doctors visited the spa, including the personal physicians to three emperors of the Holy Roman Empire. Composer Ludwig van Beethoven was a guest. Napoleon rode his horse into one of the pools, now called the Napoleon Baths.

The treatment for arthritic ailments and for those with recent orthopedic injuries consists of hot-spring and mud baths. This regime is accompanied by exercise and special diets. Years ago, visitors bathed in pits covered with mats or tree branches along the banks of the Vah River. In 1813 lodging was constructed around the springs. Privately owned until 1940, this spa is now the property of the state. The Piestany Spa has resisted commercial development and still offers a soothing, stress-free environment to visitors.

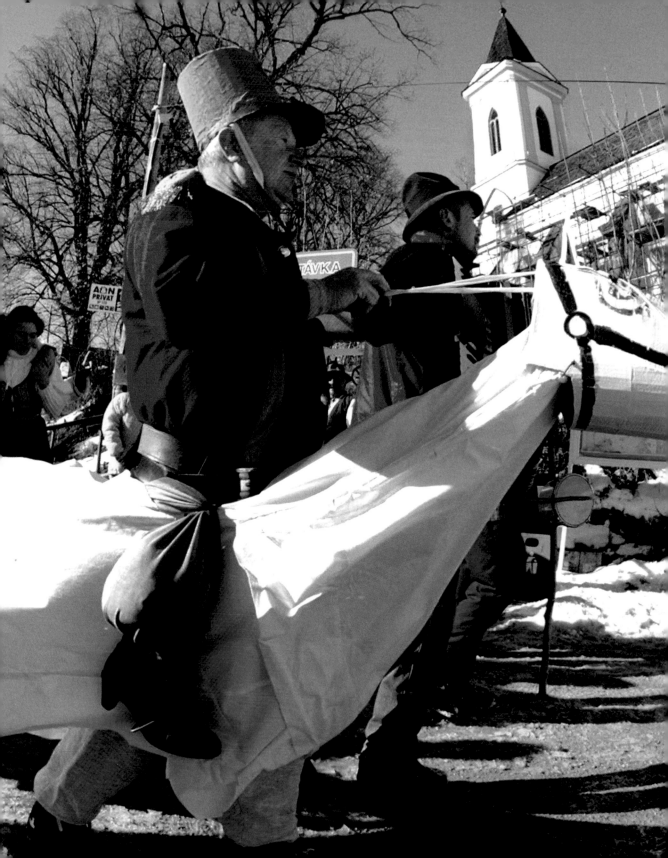

FESTIVALS

RELIGIOUS FESTIVALS are very important events in Slovakian life and are centered on significant dates in the Christian calendar. In late spring through early fall, Slovakian cultural traditions are celebrated at folk festivals held in many cities and towns.

CHRISTMAS

The observance of the Christmas season begins on December 6 with Saint Nicholas (Mikulas) Day. Children leave their shoes or boots on the windowsill and in the morning find them filled with goodies. In some areas of Slovakia, this is the traditional day for exchanging gifts, while others wait until Christmas Eve.

During the month of December, preparations for the holiday are ongoing. There are markets set up in every town with stalls selling handmade pine wreaths, wooden toys, blown-glass ornaments, hand-painted pottery, candles, firecrackers, and original watercolor paintings. Food booths at the markets sell *gulas* (GOO-lush), a stew made from venison, potatoes, and paprika; a so-called gypsy cutlet, made from grilled pork; and fresh bread spread with lard and dotted with chopped onion. *Slivovica* (SLEE-vah-vee-kuh), or plum brandy, and spiced white wine, both served hot, are traditionally enjoyed with this food.

The highlight of the Christmas celebration takes place on Christmas Eve, called Stedry Den (STEH-dree DEHN), or Generous Day. The week before, Slovakians thoroughly clean their homes and bake an enormous variety of cakes. On the evening of December 23, many people purchase a live carp that is put in the bathtub until the next morning, when the fish is killed and prepared for the evening meal. The tree is decorated on the 24th.

Protestant families often go to church in the afternoon, but Catholics attend a two-hour midnight Mass, which often has standing room only. Groups of young people and children travel from house to house singing carols, and are given pastries or apples by neighbors. When the food preparations for the evening meal are completed, many Slovakians walk in large groups to the cemetery to light candles for their loved ones.

Christmas Eve dinner is served at a table decorated with festive candles. A prayer is said, and traditionally the father of the family dips his finger in honey and makes a cross on everyone's forehead. Although the menu differs slightly depending on one's background, there is always carp, cabbage soup, and potato salad. Catholics eat a vegetarian version of the soup on Christmas Eve, while Protestants add smoked meat or sausage. After dinner, gifts are opened next to the tree.

Traditionally handpainted Easter eggs are displayed for sale near the Slovakian village of Pribylina.

A woman gets splashed with water as part of a Slovak Easter Monday custom.

Young Slovakian children do not believe in Santa Claus but are taught that baby Jesus brings the presents and angels decorate the tree. On Christmas Day, families celebrate with a big midday meal. Typical foods eaten at Christmas dinner are roast turkey, dumplings, and sauerkraut.

EASTER

The Easter holiday has an unusual combination of sacred and secular traditions. It is the most important religious festival of the year. On Palm Sunday, the week before Easter, it is customary in many villages to adorn a small tree with decorated hollow eggs and ribbons. This tree is carried from house to house by young people who sing blessings for the home and receive eggs in return.

In a tradition still followed in some farming areas, on the Thursday and Friday before Easter, fruit trees are shaken in the belief that this will produce a good crop. Cows are given fresh water so that they will provide more milk, and farmers wash themselves in the cold waters

An eager participant sells handmade *korba*, used to "whip" women's legs as part of traditional Slovakian Easter celebrations, near Pribylina.

of rivers or creeks to ensure that they will have good health for the next year. In Catholic towns, oil and candle wax are placed in front of the church and set on fire, a blaze called Judas's Fire. This custom is said to ensure a good harvest.

Slovakian Christians spend Easter Sunday in church, where they pray to mark the resurrection of Jesus Christ. After church, friends and relatives exchange decorated Easter eggs as gifts. Easter dinner is eaten in the afternoon, and consists of ham, lamb, or a kid goat. On Easter Monday, a version of an old custom to keep women "fresh" is still followed in towns and villages. Males pour or sprinkle water over females and then beat their legs lightly with a small whip made from a willow called a *korba* (KAHR-buh), while they chant blessings. Afterward the women give the men chocolates, colored eggs, and schnapps (a strong alcoholic drink). On the Tuesday after Easter, women pour water over the men who soaked them the day before.

BRATISLAVA MUSIC FESTIVAL

The Bratislava Music Festival, held in late September for two weeks, has been in existence for 40 years. The capital city is an ideal place for this festival, as it has a rich musical tradition. Haydn, Beethoven, and Liszt all performed here. It is an international festival. Musicians from 23 countries perform at its concerts. Slovakian composers of the past and present are featured. The festival emphasizes the work of talented young artists from many countries who compete for the New Talent of the Year award presented on the second day of the festival.

A Greek dance troupe performs in Bratislava during the International Folk Dance Festival.

Although the concerts are mainly chamber and orchestral, other genres, such as jazz, are included. The Slovak Philharmonic performs a work especially commissioned for the festival, and there are several premiers of works written by contemporary Slovakian composers. Festival events are promoted by posters designed by Slovakian visual artists.

FOLK FESTIVALS

Beginning in late May, cultural festivals are held in dozens of villages, cities, and towns. These festivals celebrate the music, dance, crafts, and traditional dress of the Slovakian people.

Folk costumes that are now worn and displayed at festivals were once clothes that people used everyday. A more decorated version was worn on Sundays and holidays and for important events. Although the clothes vary from region to region, the most striking feature is the colorful embroidery hand-stitched on many of the skirts, shirts, aprons, jackets, fur coats, scarves, and pants of both men and women. The traditional linen men's attire was made up of breeches (pants that end at the knee), a shirt with wide sleeves, and an apron. The women wore narrow trousers covered by a shirt without sleeves, a skirt, and an apron. Both men and women sometimes added waistcoats, blazers, belts, overblouses, and fur coats to their outfits. Married women wore a bonnet and a kerchief, while men always wore a hat, which in the colder months was made from fur.

When Slovak folk groups perform a dance at a festival, they wear the costume of the region where the dance originated. Folk songs helped to preserve the Slovak language during the years Slovakians were ruled by other countries. These songs tell of love, mourning, hope for the future, and celebration. Traditional folk dances include the Bottle Dance from the Saris region, the Cepovy from the Orava area, and the energetic Myjava from the town of the same name.

Two Slovakian participants take a break during the eighth International Festival of Ghosts and Spirits at the Bojnice Castle in 2001.

The largest festival in the Tatra Mountains, the three-day Zamagurie Folk Festival, is held in the eastern towns of Spisska Stara Ves and Cerveny Klastor in mid-June. Workshops on traditional dances and craftmaking demonstrations are given. During the festival, music and dance groups entertain enthusiastic audiences. Included is a performance by a Roma dance ensemble.

For more than 50 years, the Vychodna Folklore Festival, named after a small town in the mountainous Liptov area, has been showcasing Slovakian traditions through dances, songs, enactments of customs, and costumes from all over the country. This festival, which takes place over three days in July, has achieved national and international recognition. In addition to participants from Slovakia, the festival hosts folklore performing groups from Georgia, Croatia, Romania, and Hungary.

A group of folk musicians perform for an audience in Helpa.

FOOD

THE MAJORITY OF SLOVAKIANS eat a heavy, meat-based diet served in large portions that keeps them nourished during the long cold winters. Although the food is delicious and great care is taken with preparation, most of the dishes are very high in fat and carbohydrate. Because of decades of close contact with the Czech Republic, similar items are eaten in both countries. In Slovakia, however, the Hungarian influence has resulted in the greater use of spices.

TRADITIONAL MEALS

Many Slovakians begin their day with a home-cooked breakfast that consists of bread, butter and jam, cheese, eggs, ham or sausage, and yogurt, all washed down with tea or coffee. In the cities, commuters stop in at bakeries, where they enjoy a *kolae* (KAH-luh-eh), a pastry that is topped with cottage cheese or plum jam and poppy seeds.

Working people almost always partake of a mid-morning refreshment at a street snack bar. The most popular takeout food is the *parok* (PUH-rahk), a hot dog that is dipped in mustard or horseradish and served in a white roll. Another favorite is *langos* (LUHN-gahs), deep-fried dough smothered in garlic butter.

Although the style of cooking may vary somewhat from region to region, lunch and dinner usually begin with *polievko* (PAH-lee-ehv-kah), a hearty soup. The best-known soup is *kapustnica* (KUH-poo-stnih-cuh), made from cabbage with smoked-pork sausage, mushrooms, and plums. Two other popular soups are *fazulova polievka* (FEH-zoo-lah-vuh PAH-lee-ehv-kuh), a mixture of beans and vegetables, and *cesnakova polievka* (TSEH-snuh-kah-vah PAH-lee-ehv-kuh), a garlic soup in a chicken-broth base with parsley and egg.

The main course is usually a dish based on pork or beef, such as goulash, beefsteak, roasted pork with sauerkraut, pork chops, or spicy meatballs. Less often, roast chicken, tripe, or trout is prepared. Served with the meat or fish are potatoes, or potato or bread dumplings. The national dish, *bryndzove halusky* (BRIN-dzoh-vay HUH-loo-shkih), consists of small potato dumplings with a rich sheep's cheese sauce topped with fried pork fat. Pickled or fresh vegetable salads as well as cooked vegetables are traditional side dishes.

In many rural areas, residents have their own gardens that produce fresh fruit and vegetables during the warmer months. A summer specialty is plum dumplings, made with plums grown in Slovakia. While still warm, the dumplings are sprinkled with poppy seeds that have been mixed with sugar and melted butter. Popular desserts are cheese or apple strudel and

Traditional cheese in the Tatra Mountains.

ice cream. *Makovy kolac* (MUH-kah-vih KAH-luhk), a homemade poppy-seed cake, is another favorite. In spa towns, sweet wafers called *kupelne oblatky* (KOO-pehl-neh AH-bluh-tkih) are very popular.

In the past decade some international restaurants and fast-food pizzerias have sprung up in the larger cities. Most Slovakians, however, still rely on traditional favorites for most meals.

VEGETARIAN CHOICES

It may not be easy to be a vegetarian in Slovakia, but it is certainly possible. A traditional vegetarian dish is *vyprazny syr* (VEE-pruh-zhnee SEER), a piece of melted cheese that is fried in breadcrumbs and served with potatoes and tartar sauce. Cheese and potato omelets, fried dumplings with egg, and fried mushrooms with potatoes are the basis of other popular meatless meals. In the larger cities and towns, many restaurant menus now include a section called *bezmasite jedla* (BEHJ-meh-sih-tay YEHD-lah), which literally means without meat.

Two mushroom pickers take a rest after gathering a selection of the edible fungus from the Slovakian woods.

BEVERAGES

The legal drinking age in Slovakia is 18. Alcoholic drinks are popular and are consumed at home, in restaurants, and in pubs. Beer is considered to be the national drink of Slovakia. There are many types of beer halls. Some do not serve food, but others, called *hostinec* (HAH-stee-netch), serve basic meals along with beer. The art of beer drinking is celebrated at some festivals, where there are competitions between drinkers as to who can down the most beer the fastest.

Although the famous Czech beers are widely available, Slovakia produces many of its own local brews. The most famous, Zlaty Bazant, or Golden Pheasant, is a pilsner exported around the world. It is made

Friends at a picnic enjoy a variety of beverages with their Slovakian food.

in Hurbanovo, located in the Danube basin. Other good local beers include Topvar from Topolany, and Martiner from Martin.

Slovakia is well known for the plum brandy *slivovica* (SLEE-vah-vee-kuh), a fiery drink that is aged for three years in oak barrels. *Borovika* (BAH-rah-vee-kuh), a brandy that tastes like gin, is made in the Spis area from juniper berries. A brandy made from pears in rural areas is also a favorite.

About 2,000 years ago, the ancient Romans brought winemaking to the region that is now Slovakia, and winemaking is still an ongoing tradition. Wine-growing and winemaking take place primarily in three major areas: the southwest, the expanse between Bratislava and Trnava, and the eastern region near Mala Trna. Several Slovakian wines have won international competitions. Slovakians frequently drink locally produced wine with their meals. Many people who live in the countryside make wines and brandies for their own use and give them as gifts.

Mineral water is a widely used nonalcoholic beverage, as few Slovakians drink tap water. Popular local brands are Salvator and Baldovska. Coffee, called *kava* (KAH-vah), is drunk black and is a very strong brew served in small cups. Tea, called *caj*, is a weak beverage drunk without milk. Sour milk and *zincica* (ZEEN-tsee-tsuh), a local drink made from sheep's milk, are popular nonalcoholic choices. Slovakia is a market for imported soft drinks from many countries, and they are widely available, as are locally produced fruit juices.

Slovakians at a wine-tasting gathering.

BRYNDZOVÈ HALUSKY (POTATO DUMPLINGS WITH SHEEP'S CHEESE)

2–3 potatoes
4–5 tablespoons flour
1 egg
3 teaspoons salt
8 ounces sheep's cheese (If you cannot find sheep's cheese, feta cheese can be substituted.)
4 tablespoons milk
fried bacon, crumbled

Peel and finely shred the potatoes. Add the egg and flour. Make a dough that is not too tough but not too watery. Use more or less flour or add a bit of water to get the right consistency. Add one teaspoon of salt. Boil some water with two teaspoons of salt. Use a teaspoon to drop pieces of the dough into the boiling water. Make sure that the water is always boiling. When a dumpling, or *halusky*, is done, it will float. Pick the dumplings out with a strainer. Heat the sheep's cheese together with the milk. Stir constantly. When the liquid starts to boil, remove from heat. Pour over the dumplings and sprinkle with the crumbled bacon. Serve immediately.

MAKOVY KOLAC (POPPY-SEED CAKE)

½ cup sweet butter or margarine
1 cup sugar
6 eggs, separated
1 cup ground poppy seeds
½ cup raisins, plumped
½ teaspoon ground cinnamon

¼ teaspoon each of ground cloves and mace
grated rind of one lemon
½ cup apricot, strawberry, or raspberry jam
1 cup heavy cream, whipped

Cream the butter, add the sugar, and beat in the egg yolks. Stir in the remaining ingredients except for the jam, cream, and egg whites. Beat the egg whites, and fold into the batter. Grease and flour two 9-inch (23-cm) cake pans. Spoon half the batter into each. Bake in a 350°F (177°C) oven for 30 minutes. Let cool and remove from the pans. Spread the jam on one of the cake layers and put the other on top. Top with the cream.

POLA

CZECH REPUBLIC

Dunajec

Orava

•Zilina

ZILINA

Liptovsky
Mikulas

▲ Gerlachovsky
(8,711 ft / 2,6

•Popra

Vah

•Trencin

TRENCIN

Dumbier ▲
(6,703 ft / 2,043 m)

•Uhrovec

•Novaky

•Banska Bystrica

AUSTRIA

•Piestany

TRNAVA

•Zvolen

•Vyhne

BANSKA BYSTRICA

•Trnava

BRATISLAVA

•Modra

•Nitra

BRATISLAVA

•Sered

NITRA

•Velky
Krtis

•Diakovce

Hron

Komarno
•   Dunaj (Danube)

HUNGARY

— International boundary
— Regional boundary
● Capital city

Feet	Meters
9,900	3,000
6,600	2,000
3,300	1,000
1,650	500
660	200
0	0

N

MAP OF SLOVAKIA

ECONOMIC SLOVAKIA

Agriculture

🌽 Corn

🥔 Potatoes

🥬 Sugar Beets

🥦 Vegetables

🌾 Wheat

Natural Resources

⛑ Coal

🪵 Timber

Services

✈ Airport

🚢 Port

🧍 Tourism

🧺 Train Station

Manufacturing

🍺 Beer

◆ Cement

🏺 Ceramics

🥫 Food Products

🚚 Machinery

⚛ Nuclear Power

📦 Sugar

🧵 Textiles

🍷 Wine

ABOUT
THE ECONOMY

OVERVIEW

Slovakia has painstakingly implemented the changeover from a Communist to a free-market capitalist economy. The government has made excellent progress in stabilizing the economy and effecting structural reforms. Major industries have been privatized. Although the banks are mostly foreign-controlled, increasing foreign investment is helping to raise the standard of living.

GROSS DOMESTIC PRODUCT

US$67.34 billion (2002 estimate)

GDP GROWTH

4.4 percent (2002 estimate)

LAND USE

Arable land 30.74 percent; permanent crops 2.64 percent; others 66.62 percent (1998 estimate)

MINERAL RESOURCES

Brown coal, lignite, iron ore, copper, manganese ore, salt

CURRENCY

1 Slovak koruna (SKK) = 100 halierov
Notes: 20, 50, 100, 500, 1,000 koruna
Coins: 1, 2, 5, 10 koruna; 10, 20, 50 halierov
1 USD = 32.29 SKK (October 2004)

AGRICULTURAL PRODUCTS

Grains, potatoes, hops, sugar beets, fruit; cattle, pigs, poultry; forest products

MAJOR EXPORTS

Intermediate manufactured goods 27.5 percent, machinery and transportation equipment 39.4 percent, miscellaneous manufactured goods 13 percent, chemicals 8 percent (1999)

MAJOR IMPORTS

Machinery and transportation equipment 37.7 percent, intermediate manufactured goods 18 percent, fuels 13 percent, chemicals 11 percent, miscellaneous manufactured goods 0.5 percent (1999)

MAIN TRADE PARTNERS

European Union 49.8 percent, Germany 24.7 percent, Italy 6.4 percent, Czech Republic 15.1 percent, Russia 14.8 percent (2001)

WORKFORCE

3 million (1999)

UNEMPLOYMENT RATE

17.2 percent (2002 estimate)

INFLATION RATE

3.3 percent (2002 estimate)

EXTERNAL DEBT

US$9.6 billion (2002 estimate)

CULTURAL SLOVAKIA

Piestany Spa
People visit this ancient spa on the Vah River for its healing hot springs and mud baths.

Vychodna Festival
Folklore groups perform Slovakian customs, songs, and dances wearing traditional clothing in this three-day July festival.

Carthusian Monastery
This monastery and its original Gothic church, located at the mouth of the Dunajec gorge, were founded in the 14th century. The site is now a museum.

Bardejov
This World Heritage Site is a perfectly preserved medieval city with fortified walls, gates, and a town square. The old Jewish complex includes a synagogue and ritual bath.

Bratislava
Among the capital's landmarks are the iconic Bratislava Castle, founded in the 15th century, and the pale pink Primates' Palace, where the Treaty of Pressburg was signed in 1805.

Demanovska Caves
The Demanovska caves in the Tatra National Park form Slovakia's longest cave system. The ice cave alone is 5,742 feet (1,750 m) long. The caves attract spelunkers.

Spissky Castle
Slovakia's largest castle, near Spisske Podhradie, was founded in 1209.

Wooden Churches
The traditional wooden churches of eastern Slovakia were built without the use of nails. The Church of Saint Francis of Assisi in Hervatov is the country's oldest, built around 1500 and decorated with frescoes. The Church of Saint Michael the Archangel in Prikra was built in 1777.

ABOUT
THE CULTURE

OFFICIAL NAME
Slovenska Republica (Slovak Republic)

FLAG DESCRIPTION
Three equal horizontal bands of white, blue, and red, superimposed with the Slovak cross in a shield. The cross is white on a background of red and blue.

TOTAL AREA
18,927 square miles (49,035 square km)

CAPITAL
Bratislava

ETHNIC GROUPS
Slovak 85.7 percent; Hungarian 10.6 percent; Roma 1.6 percent (census figures under-report the Roma community, which may be as large as 380,000); Czech, Moravian, and Silesian 1.1 percent; Ruthenian and Ukrainian 0.6 percent; German 0.1 percent; Polish 0.1 percent; other 0.2 percent (1996)

RELIGIOUS GROUPS
Roman Catholic 60.3 percent, atheist 9.7 percent, Protestant 8.4 percent, Orthodox 4.1 percent, other 17.5 percent

BIRTH RATE
10.1 births/1,000 population (2003 estimate)

DEATH RATE
9.22 deaths/1,000 population (2003 estimate)

AGE STRUCTURE
0 to 14 years: 17.8 percent; 15 to 64 years: 70.5 percent; 65 years and over: 11.7 percent (2003 estimate)

MAIN LANGUAGES
Slovak (official), Hungarian

LITERACY
People ages 15 and above who can both read and write a short, simple statement related to their everyday life: 100 percent (2001 estimate)

NATIONAL HOLIDAYS
Republic Day (January 1), National Uprising Day (August 29), Constitution Day (September 1)

LEADERS IN POLITICS
Josef Tiso—premier of Nazi-controlled Slovakia (1939–45)
Alexander Dubcek—Slovak politician; introduced Prague Spring as party leader (1968–69)
Michal Kovac—first president of independent Slovakia (1993–98)
Vladimir Meciar—first prime minister of independent Slovakia (1993–94)
Ivan Gasparovic—president since 2004
Mikulas Dzurinda—prime minister since 1998

TIME LINE

IN SLOVAKIA	IN THE WORLD

1000s B.C.
Slavs settle by the Dneper River.

753 B.C.
Rome is founded.

116–17 B.C.
The Roman Empire reaches its greatest extent, under Emperor Trajan (98–17).

A.D. 400s
Slavic tribes overrun territory of modern-day Slovakia.

A.D. 600
Height of Mayan civilization

833
The Great Moravian Empire is formed.

863
Cyril and Methodius Thessaloniki convert the Great Moravian Empire to Christianity.

907
Fall of the Great Moravian Empire

1000
The Chinese perfect gunpowder and begin to use it in warfare.

1018
Slovakia is annexed by Hungary.

1400s
Saxon Germans settle in the under-populated lands of northeastern Slovakia.

1530
Beginning of trans-Atlantic slave trade.

1558–1603
Reign of Elizabeth I of England

1620
Pilgrims sail the *Mayflower* to America.

1686
The Turks are driven out of Hungary.

1776
U.S. Declaration of Independence

1789–99
The French Revolution

1861
The U.S. Civil War begins.

1867
The Austro-Hungarian monarchy is formed. Magyarization (Hungarianization) of Slovakia.

1869
The Suez Canal is opened.

1907
Hungarian becomes the official and only legal language of Slovakia.

1914
World War I begins.

1918
Fall of the Austro-Hungarian Empire. Slovakia, Ruthenia, Bohemia, and Moravia form independent Czechoslovakia.

IN SLOVAKIA	IN THE WORLD

1938
Following the Munich Agreement, Slovakia declares itself an autonomous state.

1939
Slovakia becomes an ally of Nazi Germany.

1939
World War II begins.

1944
The Slovak National Uprising

1945
The Czechoslovakian government is established at Kosice as the war winds down.

1945
The United States drops atomic bombs on Hiroshima and Nagasaki.

1948
Communists take over Czechoslovakia, with Prague as the capital.

1949
The North Atlantic Treaty Organization (NATO) is formed.

1957
The Russians launch Sputnik.

1968
Prague Spring reforms. Soviet troops march into Czechoslovakia to quash the rebellion.

1966–69
The Chinese Cultural Revolution

1986
Nuclear power disaster at Chernobyl in Ukraine

1989
The Velvet Revolution

1991
Break-up of the Soviet Union

1992
The parliament votes for independence. Vladimir Meciar is elected prime minister.

1993
Slovakia becomes an independent country.

1994–98
Meciar passes antidemocratic laws that draw heavy international criticism.

1997
Hong Kong is returned to China.

1998
Mikulas Dzurinda is elected prime minister.

1998–2002
Slovakia is beset by poor economic performance, high unemployment, and ethnic tensions.

2001
Terrorists crash planes in New York, Washington, D.C., and Pennsylvania.

2003
War in Iraq

2004
Slovakia joins the European Union.

GLOSSARY

Action K
The Communist Party's attempt, in 1950, to dismantle the Catholic Church in Czechoslovakia.

adopcia (UH-dahp-tsee-uh)
Orphaned Slovakian children.

atheism
The doctrine that there is no deity. This was the only moral doctrine permitted under Communism.

bryndzove halusky (BRIN-dzoh-vay HUH-loo-shkih)
The Slovakian national dish, consisting of potato dumplings and sheep's cheese sauce.

Czechoslovakia
The Central European country (1918–92) that was divided in January 1993 into the separate countries of Slovakia and the Czech Republic.

European Union (EU)
The organization of European countries dedicated to increasing economic integration and strengthening cooperation among its members. Slovakia joined the European Union on May 1, 2004.

fujara (FOO-yuh-ruh)
A 6-foot-long (1.8-m-long) traditional flute that is still played at folk performances in Slovakia.

goulash
A stew made with meat, assorted vegetables, and spices.

Hlinka
The pro-Nazi Slovak People's Party during World War II.

hostinec (HAH-stee-netch)
A pub that serves basic meals.

knedle (KNEH-dleh)
Dumplings.

Magyarization
Hungarianization; the program by the Austro-Hungarian Empire aimed at replacing Slovak culture and language with Hungarian equivalents.

Roma
A nomadic people originally from northern India; also known as Gypsies.

slivovica (SLEE-vah-vee-kuh)
Plum brandy.

spelunker
One who explores caves.

unos nevesty (OO-nahs NEH-veh-stee)
A wedding custom where male guests kidnap the bride and hide her from the groom.

Velvet Revolution
The six-week period in 1989, between November 17 and December 29, during which mass demonstrations brought about the bloodless overthrow of the Czechoslovakian Communist regime.

FURTHER INFORMATION

BOOKS

Axworthy, Mark W. *Axis Slovakia: Hitler's Slavic Wedge, 1938–1945*. Bayside, NY: Axis Europa Books, 2002.

Dobsinsky, Pavol. *Slovak Tales for Young and Old*. Translated by Lucy Bednar. Wauconda, IL: Bolchazy-Carducci Publishers, 2001.

Drobna, Eduard, Olga Eduard, and Magdalena Gocnikova. *Slovakia: The Heart of Europe*. Translated by Paulikova Zuzana. Wauconda, IL: Bolchazy-Carducci Publishers, 1997.

Junas, Lil. *My Slovakia: An American's View*. Burington, ON: Matica Slovenska, 2002.

Kirschbaum, Stanislav. *History of Slovakia: The Struggle for Survival*. New York, NY: St. Martin's Press, 1996.

Lazistan, Eugen, Fedor Mikovic, Ivan Kucma, and Anna Jureckova. *Slovakia: A Photographic Odyssey*. Wauconda, IL: Bolchazy-Carducci Publishers, 2001.

Leff, Carol Skalnik. *The Czech and Slovak Republics: Nation Versus State*. Nations of the Modern World Europe Series. Boulder, CO: Westview Press, 1996.

Roberts, J. M. *The Illustrated History of the World*. New York, NY: Oxford University Press, 2001.

WEBSITES

Portals to the World: Slovakia. www.loc.gov/rr/international/european/slovakia/sk.html

Central Intelligence Agency World Factbook (select Slovakia from country list). www.cia.gov/cia/publications/factbook

Banka Slovakia (Bank of Slovakia). www.basl.sk

Guide to the Slovak Republic. www.slovakia.org

Lonely Planet World Guide: Slovakia. www.lonelyplanet.com/destinations/europe/slovakia

The Slovak Republic Government Office. www.government.gov.sk/english

The Slovak Spectator (Slovakia's English-language newspaper). www.slovakspectator.sk

U.S. Department of State: Bureau of European and Eurasian Affairs: Profile: Slovakia. www.state.gov/r/pa/ei/bgn/3430.htm

FILM

Czech and Slovakia: Land of Beauty and Change. John Holod Productions, 1995.

MUSIC

Traditional Music from Slovakia. Arc Music, 2003.

Urpin Folklore Ensemble: Songs and Dances from Slovakia. Arc Music, 1999.

BIBLIOGRAPHY

BOOKS

Benes, Edvard. *Bohemia's Case for Independence*. New York, NY: Arno Press, 1971.

Korbel, Josef. *Twentieth Century Czechoslovakia: The Meanings of its History*. New York, NY: Columbia University Press, 1977.

Masaryk, Tomas Garrigue. *The Meaning of Czech History*. Chapel Hill, NC: University of North Carolina Press, 1974.

Nebesky, Richard and Neil Wilson. *Czech & Slovak Republics*. 3rd ed. London, UK: Lonely Planet Publications, 2001.

Thomson, Samuel Harrison. *Czechoslovakia in European History*. Hamden, CT: Archon Books, 1965.

Toma, Peter A. *Slovakia: From Samo to Dzurinda*. Stanford, CA: Hoover Institution Press, 2001.

Winter, Kathryn. *Katarina*. New York, NY: Farrar Straus Giroux, 1998.

WEBSITES

Slovakia: The Guide to the Slovak Republic. www.slovakia.org

Slovaks and Slovakia: Home Page. www.slovak.com

The Slovak Republic Government Office. www.government.gov.sk/english

INDEX